Anarchism

Dysophia 1

Originally published by Dysophia, UK.
in 2010

This edition published by Active Distribution
Croatia, November 2020

ISBN 978-1-914567-10-0

www.activedistribution.org

Contents

Introduction

Anarchism is more than dry political theory. It is a set of principles by which we aspire to live. It is not just about challenging the status quo, but provides tenets through which we can solve problems and (re-)define our relationships with the world around us. We shall not go into what we mean by anarchism in depth as that was covered in the first issue of dysophia. However, the basic concepts of anarchism used here are:

1 That all shall be free and equal.

2 That we extend mutual aid and solidarity (how far this should be extended is an open question...)

In this issue we look at polyfidelity and polyamory; that is, having multiple partners and lovers – something that bubbles constantly under the surface of mainstream society and within anarchist movements. Often where it does burst out into the open it is seen through the lens of traditional moral criticisms based on notions of patriarchy, ownership and attitudes to sex based more on religious morality and economic dominance than anything else.

Just as anarchism puts the power relations of economics under the microscope we should do the same for the relationships we have with our partners and lovers – often they are reflections of a society dominated by patriarchy and economic power which creates social norms that meets its own needs, not our own as individuals.

Polyamory should not wait for the anarchist utopia – it is something we can practice here and now.

Too often people are dismissed or criticised for being open with their love and sex without considering whether it is society and traditional attitudes which are at fault. At the other end of the spectrum, 'free love' is used and abused in the name of anarchism.

Thus, this pamphlet makes the links between anarchism and open relationships while also discussing how much of what currently passes as polyamory among anarchists fails to address the problems of being polyamorous within modern society, something that is often overlooked in existing literature.

Whether you are new to this subject, or already involved in open relationships there should be something for you in the following pages. If the writings here encourage you to explore the practicalities of open relationships, we hope you take away some of the lessons learned, but we strongly suggest you read some of the other resources as well, including the practical guide "With Open Hands" (see Resources at end).

If you want to contribute an article to future print runs or have strong disagreements with the politics of polyamory

as they have been set out here then please let us know.
In the meantime, take care and enjoy yourselves.

Thanks must go to the g.r.o.a.t.s., Cornerstone Housing Coop, our printers at Footprint Workers

Coop, and to all the people who contributed, proofed, commented or generally helped to get this finally off the presses and into your hands. Many people wanted their contributions to remain anonymous, but we are grateful to theirs and, indeed, everyone's contributions and those who have debated these issues over the years.

If you have comments or want to submit articles, letters, criticisms or even want to get more copies of this pamphlet, then contact us at dysophia@riseup.net Or drop us a comment on our blog at dysophia.wordpress.com

Green Anarchism and Polyamory

salmon

Anarchism is a political structure where the relationships between individuals are bound by the principles of mutual aid, freedom, equality and respect for all. There is a rejection of hierarchy, exploitation and oppression at all levels of society. Implicit in it is a confrontational attitude towards those parts of society which stand in the way of putting these principles into action, be they bosses, governments, corporations or other forms of authority.

In Green Anarchism, a strand of anarchism focused on ecological issues but much influenced by feminist, queer, liberation and animal rights philosophies, the challenge to all forms of hierarchy is extended from the workplace to all facets of one's life, which includes questioning the hierarchical notion of the human race being at the centre of political thought and action.

These principles are a powerful but accessible set of tools for analysis which fundamentally challenge us in unexpected ways.

If we wish to avoid creating or perpetuating a society where oppression is accepted in any form, then we need to take responsibility for our actions and this includes questioning our attitudes to relationships which are defined in part by the society around us.

Often what is accepted, or considered "common sense", is a pattern of behaviour instilled in us by a culture that has developed to serve those with economic power. Exploitation has never been restricted to the workplace. It extends into our personal lives, our homes and our families, and has shaped them for its own ends. Through social and religious institutions, then, later, mass media, it constantly reinforces particular notions of relationships, which we are encouraged to think of as being biologically natural, or necessary to maintain society. Witness politicians talking of "family values" as being the ideal (read faithful, productive capitalists with submissive wife to rear productive children), or how newspapers report celebrity affairs.

Part of the reason society is full of unfulfilled people, alienated from their desires and power, is because we are fed a morality on how to live and love – perfect subjects to be moulded into consumers, filling the emptiness with chocolate, fast cars, escapist television and so on. So, if modern society is force-feeding us these concepts, then we need to question them, not just because they are distractions from the creation of anarchist society, but because they are part of the fetters of control. Future societies should not be reflecting the oppressions of the past. There is no self- determination in a relationship which inherently constrains you as an individual to a way of behaving dictated by the morality of others.

In Green Anarchism a fundamental position is that, regardless of where we are coming from, our relationships with each other, sexual or otherwise, are crucial to the communities we live in. If our relationships are about control, if they stop people being free to be themselves or lead to unfulfilment, they are creating problems that will end up being replicated elsewhere in society. So, as well as changing society, we have to examine critically those things that current society has instilled in us as being 'normal' but which are actually only there to serve its needs. Thus, our personal relationships, and our approach to sex in general, issues which permeate all parts of our lives, have to be put under the spotlight of anarchism.

Modern Society

A lot has been written deconstructing how "modern, western" society has messed with our heads to give us a negative view of our bodies and of our roles within society. This is often done through tapping into desires we have for freedoms and relationships. However, the way they are presented in the media are as fantasy ideals that are unrealistic, let alone obtainable. We are encouraged to forever look for that perfect partner or a freedom which does not exist (or not without a cost). And if you cannot have it, then you are told to try harder to avoid being considered a failure.

There are, of course, markets for those who feel they have failed.

A major part of this process is to create contradictions as part of the ideal. For example, adverts often sell to men with images of sexually available women, while women are encouraged to shape themselves in the likeness of these images.

However, if they start to live up to the part of actually being sexually available they quickly find themselves the subject of criticism from yet other quarters.

With the industrial revolution came a need to regulate the labouring classes into fitting the new regimes that factories and growing cities required to function. This new order was brought about through the use of morality drawn from the Bible which sought to place married life at its heart, permitting manipulation of the population as a whole for the needs of advancing capitalism, both as workers and, later, as consumers. Sexual relationships outside marriage were considered disruptive to the working classes, so denounced as degeneracy.

The advice and imagery which continue to dominate mainstream press and drama today both echo and reinforce this morality. "Lessons" drawn from the Bible remain ingrained even when religion has been abandoned. Yet society remains obsessed with sexuality, turning it into a thing of fantasy, unobtainable and mutated away from simple pleasure. That there is so much obvious hypocrisy is a sign of how much this fraudulent morality has had to be imposed on society; it is not a natural phenomenon and repressed desires still seek expression.

How we view relationships is very much tied up with how we use our bodies. Sex and love are constantly being intertwined and "morality" is used to set limitations on what are deemed correct thoughts and behaviour, especially through the concept of marriage. "Agony aunt" pages are full of tales of infidelity and affairs that titillate or are seen as somehow naughty. It is constantly repeated or implied that sexual relations should occur within the limited parameters of monogamy and faithfulness, and that marriage with submissive, stay at home partners (in particular the women in a heterosexual relationship) is the norm encountered in popular media. Stepping outside the norm is generally accompanied with the message that it is scandalous.

This is social coercion at its worst. The notion of the family as the basic unit of society contains the implicit notion that monogamy, especially for women, and heterosexuality, is the "correct" way. Divorce still carries taints of social shame with jealousy and possessiveness accepted as normal. Sex should be contained in monogamous relationships at best and outside of the relationship is considered as "dirty", with words such as whore or slag still commonly used. This, despite the fact that the majority of adverts use the promise of sex or eroticism in some form, feeds people's repressions and generates insecurities, as irreconcilable social pressures conflict with personal needs.

Other parts of society's culture, such as pop music and soap-operas, invariably weave narratives of possessiveness into the subject of infidelity. Here, the hierarchical nature of these norms is at its most obvious, demeaning the "unfaithful" partner as an object over which there is ownership. Often there is the concept of a "betrayal" thrown in. Yet their betrayal is not to live up to the desires of the other partner in the relationship – in other words the "unfaithful" person's betrayal is to not sacrifice their needs to their original relationship! There is much less focus on the inadequacy of the original relationship in the first place.

There are other sexist subtexts going on here as well – such as when two men fight over a woman as if she has no say. Physical abuse and aggressive behaviour in the face of infidelity is then portrayed as being somehow "understandable".

More often than not there is little questioning of whether the "infidelity" is symptomatic of a larger problem in the relationship, or whether there is a need to evaluate attitudes to personal relationships as a whole. Sex and needs are subject to the false god of the monogamous relationship. Hypocritically, men get off a bit easier than women, as having affairs on the sly is often presented as an admirable prowess. These norms are further justified by the concept that there is out there the one ideal person who will be your life partner and can be the panacea of all your emotional and physical needs.

Due to this, equality and personal freedoms are rarely discussed other than in superficial terms and, in this context, commitment is mostly a surrendering of rights

over our bodies – as formalised through marriage services, where it even gets celebrated. Throw patriarchy into the mix and you have an even more disturbed system, where it is seen as acceptable that one partner should be dominant and another submissive.

Thus western society's confused attitude towards sex and a repressive concept of relationships results in the creation of a hierarchical morality, which acts as a control on people's otherwise natural desires and needs, in particular sexual ones. This morality serves capitalism far more than it serves us as individuals. That as anarchists we should challenge this should go without saying.

Only occasionally is what is written on polyamory related to anarchist principles and then much starts out with optimistic premises, as if we already live in an anarchist utopia, or that the transition will be simple. We live in one world while striving for another, so we have to deal with the conflicts this causes while balancing the competing demands of ideals and reality. The rest of this article addresses why this polyamory within anarchism is important, but points out the difficulties of challenging current norms.

Jealousy

Jealousy is a classic symptom of the dysfunctional relationships created by patriarchal and capitalist society. It is an emotion that is built around ownership. A jealous person considers that they have some sort of right over another's body or the right to have the sole emotional relationship with them; the needs and feelings of that other person become secondary to the desires of the jealous person. Thus it is an emotion that dehumanises and disrespects others. It treats individuals as property – just like capitalism and other authoritarian economic-political systems do.

Jealousy is also an expression of insecurity, which implies that there is power imbalance going on in the relationship, that people's needs and desires are not being met in a way that is respectful to all, or that there is a need for control over them which negates their personal choices and freedoms. It is a natural emotion as well, for example when the nature of a relationship changes and one partner seeks to withdraw.

None of this takes away from the fact that if someone chooses to not have a sexual or emotional relationship with you, that is their right. A relationship under anarchist agreement should be a set of mutual understanding, not built on demands and unvoiced expectations. Likewise, if they consider that to fulfil all their needs they want more than one relationship, then why should that not be their right?

Often jealousy is embedded in principles of patriarchy as well. Take for example the situation when a woman leaves one man for another, the jilted partner takes his anger and frustration out on the new lover, blaming him for the end of the relationship. This is lessening of the role the woman, in this particular situation, as it demeans her ability to make choices for herself and implicitly assumes that her pleasure and needs are less important than the man's. This is classic patriarchy though it is easy to see how this applies to other scenarios of all gender mixes. The use of language, that a partner has somehow been 'stolen' is indicative of how this type of relationship has been cast in the forge of capitalist practice.

Jealousy is the antithesis of freedom, equality or solidarity. Anarchist principles point out that when it comes to an intimate relationship between two consenting adults the two individuals must be treated as equals in all ways. Their choices are to be respected. Of course it is not going to be easy – there is a lot of indoctrination to overcome. The key to avoiding jealousy is communication on a number of levels and all parties involved attempting to understand the needs and desires of their partners. It can be a difficult first step, but it makes a big difference to step back and consider the other person's needs and desires.

It is a powerful realisation of anarchist principles when you actively place a partner's needs as being on a par with your own, to accept that you do not have to be everything for them at all times, or them for you. Likewise, that you have your own freedoms which should be met. Ask yourself how realistic or even possible it is that one person should fulfil all of your desires, and whether expecting that of them is fair. It is an expectation that you would reject if imposed on you.

Likewise, as anarchists we should challenge jealous behaviour in our friends.

"Ethical Meddling"

Getting involved in our friends relationships is sometimes more challenging than intervening through, say direct action, but it is more easy to make time to go gently about it. If we fear for the relationship health of our friends, we should tell them with specific care, and offer them space to reflect on what is happening. Such offers should be opportunities for them to tell us we're just projecting our own concern about ourselves and our own relationships! See also the article "A Personal Journey" later in this booklet.

Polyamory and Polyfidelity

So, accepting that there is a right to determine who you have relationships with, or who you sleep with, or even how many, where does this get you?

This is a big question - there are so many variations in the types of relationships that are now open to you. What matters is that you make the choices freely and that you treat those you involve in your relationships with the respect they deserve as another equal person.

There are many phrases and words used to describe having multiple emotional and/or physical relationships. We shall stick to a few for convenience, in particular "polyamory" and "polyfidelity". Polyfidelity means being faithful to more than one person. For most people, however, there is likely to be a mixture of relationship types, so polyamory, that is, having multiple lovers, covers most bases. This is not to say they are mutually exclusive. Often people simply refer to having open relationships – we will use all three interchangeably though.

However, there is far more to it than simply declaring that you are having an open relationship. Even if you are lucky to move in polyamorous anarchist circles there are right and wrong ways to go about it. Also, as an individual, you need to consider what your needs actually are. There are two primary approaches to develop your concept of open relationships.

Fulfilment

The first notion is that of fulfilment; that is, understanding that the needs and desires a person has are relatively unlikely to be met by one person alone. It is not necessarily reasonable for one person to be all things for another person all of the time. We have to get on with our own lives as well, and as humans our desires change over time.

If you love someone, if you care for them as an equal, then surely what you want for them is to have a fulfilling life where as many as possible of their desires can be reasonably met. The issue is about the respect you have for your partner rather than about your requirements. This is not to say that your needs should not be met, but that you are part of a balancing exercise. It cannot be one-way demands and expectations. You have to treat your lover as an equal in emotional and physical needs.

Simply understanding that a partner is fulfilling their jigsaw of needs with different people (sexual or otherwise) and that this is actually a positive thing is a good first step on the way to a working open relationship. This is not to say that fulfilment cannot be achieved with one person, but if it is not happening, then there is no reason to end up feeling trapped in a closed relationship. It's not healthy.

Underlying this is a principle of sharing and offering, of understanding our partners' needs and choices, rather than demanding that they conform solely to your desires. Fulfilment is not just about sex, but about all the different aspects that a relationship involves for you.

In this situation, what matters is what each of you brings to your relationship, and an acceptance that because your partner is with others does not mean they love you any less. Conventional society is quick to tell us that 'infidelity' is a problem; yet most of those who are in healthy open relations will happily tell you that relationships are often greatly strengthened by that very openness and the acceptance that partners are simply fulfilling their desires rather than betraying the relationship.

Related to this is the concept that one person can be all things for another, something often taken for granted without justification. Some relationships work very successfully on this level, but every relationship has degrees of give-and-take and compromise required to make it work. However, clearly many people want/need more than what one person can reasonably give. As individuals we need to question our assumptions that we are perfect with the necessary time, talents and capabilities to demand monogamy of another.

As anarchists we should query the hierarchies implicit in our conceptions of ourselves and how, in turn, we replicate those hierarchies through our relationships, in particular through asking others to give up some of their freedoms on our behalf.

In other words, to put it a little plainly, our insecurities are more our problem than other people's. And while relationships are an important part of dealing with them, the first port of call should be with ourselves, not making demands of others that restrict them more than they are comfortable with. Emotional blackmail is grim stuff.

Emotionally oriented relationships

The other approach is to remove sex as a defining principle of a relationship, because what matters is the personal connection between two people. This approach used to be much more common, but it is rarely considered in a world where sex permeates every form of entertainment and advertising.

Sex is important, but its role in relationships has been greatly distorted in the world of mass media. Indeed, sex has become one of the major dialectical arenas whereby the capitalist need for consumerism distorts in turn attitudes to sex and even what sex means. This commodification of eroticism is a relatively new phenomenon in terms of human relationships, but a potent one.

So, it is useful to step back and examine how much our choices and needs have been shaped by a world were sex is pre-eminent and intimacy has to be measured by it. What is to stop us rejecting its dominance altogether? This is not a call to celibacy, but to give greater prominence to all the other needs and desires that relationships serve to fulfil.

Back to anarchism

It is easy to dismiss sex and relationships as having little to do with radical social change, yet how often do we hear of divides in radical groups because a couple split up. They have fallen into classic patriarchal/capitalist definitions of ownership over individuals without realising – and the fact they've split is probably a good thing as they have such screwed up approaches to hierarchy and control. It is a basic thing to mess up on, and often demonstrates more fundamental flaws within a group's critiques. Inter-personal relationships are just as fundamental to anarchist politics as anything else.

For all that you may have a revolutionary workplace ready to challenge the forces of the state and the bosses, if it is still a place of prejudice and personal repressions it is simply replicating the power relations of capitalism, imperialism, etc.

These oppressions are not constrained to the workplace – it is obvious there is a correlation between what happens in our workplace and what happens in wider society. Thus, anarchism is also about being political in our personal lives, opening our eyes to the hidden power-structures that exist in everyday relationships and critiquing them.

Being aware of power-dynamics in our personal relationships helps us understand them in the wider world and to see how society uses them to constantly reinforce convention. We can see the daily manipulation to which people are subjected in magazines, adverts, on television and so on.

If our personal relationships are being used to keep us in conformity with the current system, then to challenge the basis of our relationships is part of tackling the political dead end that the mainstream continually tries to force us down. It is easy to talk about challenging the system and forget about challenging ourselves at the same time. It is not about putting one above the other, but realising that both have to go hand in hand to be truly revolutionary.

Our personal and sexual relationships are a very obvious place to start. Of course there are many other aspects to anarchism and relationships, but for the purposes of this booklet this is our focus.

The Red and Black Movement

The importance of the 'worker's struggles' is often used to justify ignoring other issues such as patriarchy, including personal and sexual relationships. In this vacuum it is no surprise that capitalism and western mores slip in to dictate the nature of relationships within these movements.

Often having multiple partners or open relationships is dismissed as being middle- class decadence. But what is not being admitted is a willingness to discard prized notions of liberty in favour of otherwise discredited systems when faced with the challenge of personal change. This is a paucity of critique.

"The "decadence" criticism may be related to tendencies among activists to work themselves into the ground. Deliberately making time for more love and relaxation, and less work and consumption, is often a sensible change for per-

sonal sustainability. Though it does meet resistance from hard-working friends who cannot imagine taking time out for themselves in this way. Making time is not just about having new lovers but very much about improving relationships we are already in, and keeping up-to-date with how we are feeling."

Putting it into practice

Let's get beyond the various myths of what open relationships are all about. Firstly it is not just about being able to sleep around as if it has no impact on the rest of our relationships. Freedom is not something to be abused and every relationship has at least two people in it whose needs must be balanced.

We have to ensure that the choices we give ourselves and partners (however temporary the relationship) are not controlling, misleading or abusive.

Not a panacea

Open relationships do not mean an end to all the pains that come with relationships, but they can be a way to see that the change is a positive thing, even if it hurts us in the present.

Relationships change because you have two people in them who are constantly changing. It is not unnatural to have them drift apart over time, to find others more in tune with where they are right now and so on. But this is also a strength of polyamory – it is about them being happy, and you being open to that. Furthermore, it is not necessarily the end of your own relationship with that person, simply a moving on to a different place for it.

However, while jealousy is insecurity without foundation, not all insecurity is misplaced. Where there is a foundation for it, it is essentially grief for what is being lost. It hurts to lose your primary, and to see them moving onto someone else for the same relationship as you had is quite likely to rub salt in the wound. Relationships do come to an end of their own accord, albeit often because there has been a lack of transparency or communication somewhere along the line over what one or both of the partners want.

If it is you who is moving on, there is also an onus to acknowledge that you are changing, that what you want is now different and not to hold on to the illusion of a relationship when it is no longer true.

Agreements

All relationships come with implicit agreements or rules. Even if we do not have them explicitly spelled out in our heads – not murdering a partner is a common rule, though they come in much more subtle forms such as how much time you expect your partner to spend with you. Even when explicit, each partner may have a different understanding of what they are.

This need not be a problem, and nor is it against the principles of anarchism. What matters is that they are mutually agreed and respected. Talking them out gives each person a reasonable impression of where they stand with each other, and what they can honestly expect to be asked of them. This does not mean they will not change, but if they do, then that should be acknowledged. It saves a lot of hurt in the long run.

Choice

Uninformed choice is no choice. Freedom and equality require honesty to work and you cannot build an honest relationship on false foundations. People need to know where they stand with you, and if you are too cowardly or self-absorbed to explain the situation fully to them, then you are acting out a gross betrayal. To lie to someone, or mislead them about your offers and intentions removes the possibility of clear, informed choice and shows that you do not respect them.

This works both ways, if you are not happy with your relationship, whether open or closed, then you need to say so and talk it through. Suppressing your own desires without acknowledgement is a lie that only serves someone else's control.

Predators

Unfortunately, there are those who prey on vulnerable and inexperienced people and call it polyamory. We all need to watch and challenge this. Too many people have been lost to activist movements because they have been sucked in by those with an agenda putting self-gratification first but justify it in the name of "free love" and the like.

Victims often feel used and unable to turn to the rest of the social group, who may have close friendships with the predator. Often these predators are good activists in other arenas or personally charming, but that does not excuse their behaviour. To not challenge it amounts to condoning it. If we would not tolerate physical abuse why should we tolerate emotional abuse? None of us are very good at this, and few of us have practice at challenging our friends, but it is something anarchists need to work on in general.

Health and safety

It is your responsibility to take care that you are not endangering your partners, especially if you are not using protection. Be careful what you do, and take care. A cavalier attitude is potentially dangerous as well as being highly disrespectful. This is one of the issues you should discuss openly with your various regular partners. When it comes to casual sex there is no excuse not to be protected.

Marriage

Is marriage dead in polyamorous anarchism? Not in the slightest. Marriage is a commitment between two (or even more) individuals at its most basic level. On top of this has been tacked a lot of patriarchal/capitalist-oriented ritual which can easily be disposed of.

In anarchism there is nothing to stop you making a commitment (marriage or hand- fasting if you like) completely on your own terms. It can be as open, and involve as many people as you desire. In anarchism, there is no need for the sanction of a state or church, so it becomes simply a statement of intent, and, if appropriate, can involve the whole community as well.

Secondary/Primary relationships

No two of your relationships are going to be the same (what would be the point?). It is therefore useful to acknowledge that different relationships are likely to be given different levels of importance. One person may have multiple relationships, of which one is of particular significance and importance for them, that is, a primary.

Everyone else (probably) is a secondary. This is not necessarily something that has to be negative, but it is always important to be clear about it. We should point out that there is no clear definition of what a prime relationship is, so some people reject it on that basis. As a friend has said:

> *"... any definition (lover, primary, secondary, wife, husband...) is in danger of becoming a limitation over time. Human beings are alive in the fluid tension between wanting to belong/be secure/have community, and to explore/be free/creative/individuals. That tensi-*

on exists in all of us, and we make these abstract pulls concrete, in part by the changing promises and deeds we make within our relationships. Perhaps it feels too difficult or awkward to keep up with our changing feelings, and vocalise these changes. But if we do not at least acknowledge uncertainties or change as they grow, then we are falling into deceit."

However, Primary, etc, are useful concepts which remain in enough common currency to make them worth discussing. Ultimately, we suspect, everyone will come to their own definitions if they find these terms useful. Just be clear abo-ut what they mean to your partners.

Polyamory recognises that primary relationships do not have everything the partners need, and that secondary re-lationships are a method of fulfilling the remaining desires. Where it often falls down is in situations where a relation-ship blurs these lines, that is, one where someone has more than one relationship for which they are primary. In these situations the secondary partners will not have the emoti-onal support from having a primary partner to themselves. Knowing what you can reasonably give is vital, and being clear and open will prevent it slipping into an emotionally destructive process.

Another issue where problems arise is when the nature of the relationships change and, for whatever reasons, a se-condary relationship becomes a primary one in place of the original one. These changes can give rise to issues of jealousy because what was a comfortable situation is no longer there and insecurities arise. Again, communication is the only way around this. Polyamory is not a cure for all the pain that relationships give rise to.

However, it needs to be acknowledged that within all of this there is a hierarchy of relationships and this is a challenge within itself as well as to anarchist beliefs. It would be ideal if this were not the case, especially as this binary in itself sets up its own rigid concepts, but sometimes you have to be practical about it as there are so many factors that come into play here, from our own changing needs, to geography and so on. Not recognising hierarchies opens the door to misunderstandings about the nature of a relationship – in particular, we would say, where sex and deep emotional support are defining factors.

This is still an area of open debate as it is heavily dependent on context, and it is worth reading "With Open Hands" for an alternative perspective.

Ageism

A criticism that is levelled at polyamory (though it exists outside of it as well) is the number of relationships with a large age gap, especially between an older man and younger woman. This is a valid criticism, but often it is based on the wrong set of premises, more informed by conventional mores and often displaying an implicit sexism.

Every relationship should be approached on the basis of the individuals concerned and the power-dynamic between them. Ageism can work both ways.

What matters is whether there is a history of abusive/manipulative relationships by one of the individuals, such as someone who turns inexperience into emotional dependence, or uses their reputation to seduce. Rather than sniping, the best thing is to talk to the individuals and check that they are as comfortable with the situation as they seem to be.

Exploring different kinds of sexuality

There is an opportunity in non-monogamy to challenge ourselves on different levels, that is, to experiment with different types of sexuality and sexual personalities. It can be a useful and interesting thing to do. What one partner may not be comfortable with or interested in exploring another can be excited to help with. It can also be a very interesting personal experience which allows us to challenge our own concepts of ourselves and our identities.

It is also important to respect that people have made their own choices in relation to their sexuality. If they are not comfortable outside that zone, then as long as they do not consider you any the less or different as an individual, that is their privilege and should be respected.

Promiscuity

There is nothing wrong in sex for the sake of sex as long as all those who are involved know where they stand. It is not acceptable to seduce someone who is clearly looking for more out of an encounter simply for personal gratification. On the other hand if all you want is a no-strings attached encounter, then be up- front about it. As ever, the way to avoid hurting people is to be clear about where they stand...

"I've been generally promiscuous fairly consistently over the last few years, and am now moving away from it, because it's a bit too much like eating sweets when you need a square meal, but I also don't like feel that having one-night-stands affects these secondary relationships much.

Though a basic suggestion for people in primary relationships going casually on the pull is: Yes, you should have that conversation about being in a primary relationship in the evening and not the following morning, however unsexy you feel it is.

The person you are pulling may not be just looking for a one-night stand, or even a secondary relationship, and they should be given the choice. And it's NOT their responsibility to ask, especially given the way you've been chatting them up, which suggests you've not had a shag for months and they're the love of your life..., and so on."

A personal perspective

anon

The main issues polyamory has raised for me are those around power, hierarchy and control (slotting in to my views as an anarchist), self-reflection, awareness, care and compassion (helping me learn how best to behave).

Power

The thing about anarchism, is that there's no end product. We'll never get to our anarchist utopia and say "We've arrived. Let's relax." because power and hierarchy and control and domination will always be there and need watching and discussing and dismantling on whatever micro or macro scale.

Polyamory is an opportunity to learn more about power, to help us keep on our guard against its abuse, and can even give us some practice at challenging it.

What I've learnt about power is that it's difficult to see it when you have it. My black/working class/queer/female friends have a way better understanding of it through their own experiences than white, middle class me. I may be female, but I've been pretty much cushioned from patriarchy by my other privileges. I've only started noticing it when I started opening my eyes to other people's oppression.

This means that power can be pretty hard to get your head around as a white male. You might think it's not there. It probably is.

Patriarchy means that women are socialised to meet men's needs. To the men who have an emotional reaction to that statement: I'm not saying you ask for this. I'm not saying you are contributing to it. I hope you're not. And I hope that by being as aware of it as possible, you can try not to benefit from it. But it is there. That's how it works. If you haven't noticed how you are benefiting from it, you certainly are.

This tendency for both men and women to focus on meeting men's needs is just one of the aspects of patriarchy that gives men more power to their elbow. So when blokes are with a woman who is much younger than them, I advise much vigilance. I've caused anger bringing this up with people in the past. After suggesting that someone should keep an awareness of their power, I was told I was out of order.

We need to let each other help us to be vigilant. I would have been happy to have been told, "I think about it lots. I just don't want to discuss it with you." I was sceptical when instead I got, "It's not an issue here."

I've heard men express their sense of a lack of power given their younger lover is gorgeous and could leave them at any moment. I'm not quite sure that that isn't just insecurity rather than powerlessness.

Yes, sexual power is a real source of power for some women. Indeed, in some cultures, it's pretty much the only source of power that women have. And it's definitely more of a 'power over' rather than 'power with' type of power. It can be used carelessly. It can leave lovers hurt. However, sexual power is just one source of power. In a couple's day-to-day negotiations, such as on what to do at the weekend or the boundaries of their relationship, age and gender may be more relevant. Keep a look out. Who gets their way more?

There are many factors which can affect the power balance between two people: age, gender, who finds it easier to pull, who is more comfortable with themselves, confidence, who finds it easier to connect with other people, how much of a priority you are to the other person. It is fairly likely power imbalances will be present within a relationship, although they may ebb and flow. Do you pay them attention?

A crucial reason to keep an eye on power dynamics with your lovers, is that poly relationships have a great potential to damage people.

If someone is anyway feeling a little low on the self-esteem front, consider the effect these situations may have:

1.Comparing yourself to your lover's other lovers.
2. Your lover choosing to be with someone else in a social situation.
3.Being told your lover is in love with someone else.

These situations can seriously undermine people's self-confidence. And their struggle to cope when they believe they should be able to cope can undermine it even further. If they have the right support & care, and are able to express their hurt when they need to, there can be great opportunities to learn and grow.

If they feel it's really uncool that they are struggling so much with being poly, and think their lover will like them less if they show themselves to be uncool, damage is more likely.

As a lover of someone struggling, maybe you don't really want to hear about their hurt. If you listened, the flipside of their hurt could be your guilt. And a common poly way to deal with guilt seems to be to will it away with self-righteousness. "That's who I am." "They just need to deal." Well, a big help for their dealing could be your listening. Ideally non-judgementally and without guilt (cos it's not all about you anyway. Be careful that you don't make it so).

Hierarchy

When I was single, I experienced being a secondary/tertiary/of-no-meaning to others. Being generally way more up for a lasting connection than whoever I was sleeping with, this was of limited fun.

I find the hierarchical nature of primary relationships difficult in anarchist terms.

Decisions on how to spend time and who to give attention to are based on past history and status, and not on humanity and need. I experienced needing support at a time when a lover was barely acknowledging my existence in the presence of their primary.

Defining your lovers as primary & secondaries can be done either prescriptively or descriptively. Either you are stating, “This lover will always be my priority,” or you are describing the fact that you hang out loads/live together.

I understand why someone would want to be prescribed as a primary. People’s need for security is something that can be worked on (gently, ideally at the pace of the slowest). But saying to someone you are sleeping with, “You will always be less of a priority to me than X”, sucks.

There is also the thorny issue of how polyamory may affect the informal hierarchies within a group. According to Jo Freeman’s essay ‘The Tyranny of Structurelessness’, informal hierarchies are determined by friendship groups. Sexual relationships strengthen friendships and alliances, and the result of some people’s sense of belonging in a community, is often other people's exclusion and alienation. In the following article, 'Let them eat cake', this sense of exclusion is clearly expressed.

Where polyamory is more the norm, social occasions are perhaps more likely to be sexually charged, what with all the flirting and pulling intentions of those present.

I know of people who have avoided social occasions because they are not comfortable in such a sexualised space. This may be because they are temporarily depressed, have longer-term self-esteem issues, or simply do not want to be around such behaviour.

Being physically attractive is one more source of privilege and power. People are more likely to want to be your friend, and to listen to you (see studies on physical appearance and earning power). Those deemed to be less attractive, and those who chose not to relate to others on a sexual level, may already be less well listened to in their political groups. (If you are thinking of examples where this is not the case, notice the gender/age/experience of those exceptions. Of course there are other sources of power.) If people do not wish to attend parties to watch other people pull, they will be missing out on the social connections which would strengthen their part in the group.

Please be mindful of how your sexual energy and polyamory may alienate and exclude.

Control

Control is an issue in all relationships. Part of my motivation for not being monogamous is that I'd observed my tendency to nag and control in a previous relationship, and I wanted to have a clear sense of my partner as an individual: Free of me and of my beliefs on what she or he should be doing.

So maybe it can be less of an issue in polyamorous relationships than monogamous ones. After all, you're letting go of that "you can only sleep with me" rule, so you can hope the rest will follow. It doesn't always, so it also needs to be watched.

Some people are 'alphas'. They characteristically have ideas, take initiative, and help the rest of us get organised.

Some alphas operate in the realm of 'power with'. They might lead a collective process of organising. They may facilitate a group decision. Other use 'power over', taking control in ways that help their ideas to happen, or their needs to be met.

Some alphas share the characteristic commonly observed in other species. They have lots of lovers and lots of sex.

So especially if you have an alpha for a lover (or friend), keep an eye on the way they navigate between 'power with' and 'power over'. Notice when any control is being used on you, and call them out for it.

Self-reflection & Awareness

It's part of the joy of polyamory that the more relationships you have, the more people you get to learn from, and the more practice you get at behaving well.

We all have insecurities. How careful can we be to take them on ourselves and not let them restrict others?

Fluidity of roles is meant to be an indicator of a healthy relationship. When you are in more than one relationship, contrasts can give you more perspective on how entrenched your behaviour might have got with a particular lover, and what limiting beliefs you might have about yourself/your lover/your relationship which keep that behaviour going. Juicy learning.

Of course, there's a balance to strike between work on yourself (aka navel-gazing) and work out in the wider world. Relationships can take up lots of attention and this draws your attention away from being useful to others outside of your relationships.

Care and compassion

When I started my current relationship, it was non-monogamous, in that my boyfriend was the main focus. Then I fell suddenly, unexpectedly, deeply in love with someone else. I realised, "So this is polyamory." and it got quickly messy. It was not a good time for my boyfriend. Polyamory was not part of our deal. But I had a week of new relationship energy, and naive optimism about what a bright, love -filled future I had. I couldn't see past my own euphoria.

I was excited about how the whole polyamory theory was working for me in practice. My new-found love made my love for my boyfriend feel even brighter and deeper. Sure, it was bringing up some difficult issues in our relationship. But they were issues, now in the open, that we finally had the momentum to tackle. Yey. All brilliant. For me.

Meanwhile the boyfriend - hurt, insecure, confidence shaken - was shocked by my lack of empathy and care. As I was coming down from the new-romance high, comments from friends like,

"Put yourself in his shoes." finally started to sink in. I was amazed by how much I hadn't. And the day I started to open my eyes to where the boyfriend was at (by this point, fairly broken), was the same day I realised I'd have to let my other love go for now.

My boyfriend says it pains him that he's stopping me doing something I feel for. So I know he's not going to take the piss. He'll put the effort into building up his confidence so one day I can be non-monogamous again, and hopefully go on to polyamory. I'm now focused on creating a safe space for that journey. It may take years. Hopefully not too many.

Let them eat cake: Anarchist polyamory theory and reality

This piece of writing is not intended to make any statement about what types of sexual relationships are appropriate for humans. Nor is it intended to make any statement about the nature, essential or otherwise, of the categories of gender or sexual orientation. It is a record of my experience of how anarchist theories of polyamoury have functioned socially and ideologically in a particular context. I do not apologise if the things I have uncovered are unpleasant. I find them unpleasant too.

I would like to break away from the heady spiralling exchange of standard abstractions and stereotyped responses, most of which are entirely imaginary, and have a look at what is actually going on at ground level.

My experience in this context has been that the theories are used to help create a high-flying and exclusive social and sexual scene that promotes itself as a universal model. Certain groups of people who preach anarchist values aspire to the decadent lifestyle of the aristocracy with its unmoderated hedonism, drug use and sexual activity.

The exclusive network functions as an in-group defined by, among various other more or less obscure things, access to the open relationship 'circuit' (their word, not mine). The exclusivity of the in-group is very efficiently defended by denial of its existence. An unfortunate outsider who makes the embarrassing error of attending an in-group social function, cynically advertised as open to all, will find the flamboyant sexual manoeuvrings of the in-group constantly flaunted in their face. At the same time as they are excluded, they will be told in endless repetitive pamphlets that the wonderful world of anarchist swinging is open to everyone, implying that if you're excluded from it then you must be exceptionally inadequate.

In-group dominant heterosexual males are those who have dedicated tremendous effort to perfecting their sub-cultural conformity and pulling technique. The arbitrary rules of anarchist sexual competition allow them to compete more or less covertly with out-group males while denying that they are so doing: how could there be sexual competition when everything is open to everyone? Since membership of the 'circuit' is an important marker of social status, this allows them to dominate out-group males not only in sexual competition but also socially. The out-grouper, if he has dedicated his energy to more worthwhile tasks than learning how to pull anarchist women, or if he finds it distasteful to compete in defence of his sexual territory, may be successfully humiliated by the superior social status, unscrupulousness and more practised seduction and competition techniques of the dominant in-grouper. For a heterosexual male, exclusion from the sex circuit (whether he is interested in it or not) throughout-competition by an in-group dominant male is equivalent to exclusion from the social network, or at least to low status. The options available to him are to leave the entire situation, to accept low social status, or to join the competitive frenzy and attempt the tedious and pointless business of learning the appropriate arbitrary social codes and competitive techniques when he'd much rather be spending his time and effort learning acoustic blues guitar. Of course similar processes occur in all kinds of cultural contexts, but in this case they are particularly highlighted by the frantic atmosphere of courting and competition and by the depressing hypocrisy of the in-group and its ideological emissions.

Here is a detailed example of how it works, in the context of heterosexual relationships, to which my experience is limited (which I have been told by a hardline in-grouper, along with my gender, makes anything I say worthless). At an in-group function I foolishly attended, I was having a conversation with a woman with whom I was in a serious sexual love relationship. A well-known in-group dominant male appeared, sat behind her and started vaguely massaging her shoulders while talking loudly and smoothly about sex as if he were a great expert on the subject. His behaviour was clearly grossly offensive, for its poor taste and lack of subtlety if nothing else. The woman, who was immersed in the process of becoming socially involved with the network, went along with it and colluded with him in excluding me from the interaction. I did not have the usual recourse of complaining about the offensive behaviour of the leering groping anarchist stud, to whom I represented nothing more than a minor obstacle between his looming cock and its target of the minute, without being accused of the deadly sin of jealousy by my then partner. In mainstream culture – I mention it only to provide perspective - his behaviour would be regarded as highly insulting. In some cultural contexts it would be taken as a deliberate provocation to violence. In the distorted mirror fantasy world of anarcho-swinger culture it is not only acceptable but commendable, and the one who suffers the social attack is in the wrong because the dominant one can both deny that he is being competitive and accuse the other of jealousy. Clearly this is to the advantage of in-group dominant males. It was particularly upsetting that my partner colluded enthusiastically and self-righteously with the in-group male's negation of my existence – symbolic killing - in order to further her status in the network. The crucial point is that she was able to validate their behaviour using the anarcho- polyamourist ideological construct, effectively denying that she had any responsibility for her behaviour towards me despite our having been in a serious relationship for a significant time. The validation of their behaviour, and the corollary invalidation of my objection to it, were not only theoretical but also social, as the whole crowd of high-flyers danced merrily on their way for the rest of the event leaving me hurt, angry and isolated. The theory allowed my partner and her suitor to treat me as if I was nothing, as they colluded in gluing another brick into the wall of exclusivity with their body fluids.

These are some of the most thoroughly unpleasant, hypocritical and devious behaviours I have witnessed. It seems to me that many people are just reciting the empty liturgy of open relationship theory dogmas and not talking about their real emotions at all, much less considering the real emotions of others. Frequently, past responses to my arguments have been mindless repetitions of the open relationship catechism, with no real independent self-reflection. The thing is largely a pathologically euphoric theoretical fantasy.

One of the most disastrous existential errors a person can make is to think that they are what they think they ought to be.

Now, if a bunch of upper middle class luvvies want to smugly fuck each other to save the world, that's their business. What I find truly objectionable is the way the dishonest and decadent inner values of the network are advertised in books, pamphlets and workshops. Looking at an anarchist textbook on open relationships, I find photos of young, attractive, tattooed, Californian cutesy-punks, a story about how the author's primary partner went to a party and pulled someone, and the helpful suggestion that one should consider having a shower when going straight from one person's bed to another's. What does that have to do with my life? I've been to about three parties in the past ten years. I go to bed at ten o'clock and spend two hours a day doing meditation and internal martial arts training. It's highly unlikely that I would go to a party and pull someone. And even I am relatively young, fit, healthy, counter-culturally articulate and so on. What on earth does this stuff have to do with, for example, someone middle-aged, poor, depressed, uneducated, overweight and disabled? There are very many people who simply do not have the opportunity to have sexual experiences with others. For the precious high-flyers of the open relationship circuit to flaunt and publicly analyse their extravagant sexual and social lives in this way is like walking up to someone who's starving, stuffing a big slice of cake in your mouth, and complaining about how eating too much cake makes you feel sick.

Author's note: This article has appeared in various versions and I have received many comments. Some were supportive and confirmed the accuracy of my observations. Others were more neutral, or pointed out certain more or less serious flaws. Some, however, resorted either to restating the tired pious dogmas of anarcho-polyamourism without attempting to answer the main points I was making, or to personal insults implying that the commenter is getting their end away more than me and is therefore in a better position of sociological observation. I hope this preamble will pre-empt both of those responses and compel those who for some reason wish to argue against me to address what I am actually saying.

http://sourmangopowder.blogspot.com

Emma Goldman on
MARRIAGE AND LOVE

The popular notion about marriage and love is that they are synonymous, that they spring from the same motives, and cover the same human needs. Like most popular notions this also rests not on actual facts, but on superstition.

Marriage and love have nothing in common; they are as far apart as the poles; are, in fact, antagonistic to each other. No doubt some marriages have been the result of love. Not, however, because love could assert itself only in marriage; much rather is it because few people can completely outgrow a convention. There are today large numbers of men and women to whom marriage is naught but a farce, but who submit to it for the sake of public opinion. At any rate, while it is true that some marriages are based on love, and while it is equally true that in some cases love continues in married life, I maintain that it does so regardless of marriage, and not because of it.

On the other hand, it is utterly false that love results from marriage. On rare occasions one does hear of a miraculous case of a married couple falling in love after marriage, but on close examination it will be found that it is a mere adjustment to the inevitable. Certainly the growing-used to each other is far away from the spontaneity, the intensity, and beauty of love, without which the intimacy of marriage must prove degrading to both the woman and the man. Marriage is primarily an economic arrangement, an insurance pact. It differs from the ordinary life insurance agreement only in that it is more binding, more exacting. Its returns are insignificantly small compared with the investments. In taking out an insurance policy one pays for it in dollars and cents, always at liberty to discontinue payments. If, however, woman's premium is a husband, she pays for it with her name, her privacy, her self-respect, her very life, "until death doth part." Moreover, the marriage insurance condemns her to life-long dependency, to parasitism, to complete uselessness, individual as well as social. Man, too, pays his toll, but as his sphere is wider, marriage does not limit him as much as woman. He feels his chains more in an economic sense.

Thus Dante's motto over Inferno applies with equal force to marriage: "Ye who enter here leave all hope behind."

That marriage is a failure none but the very stupid will deny. One has but to glance over the statistics of divorce to realize how bitter a failure marriage really is. Nor will the stereotyped Philistine argument that the laxity of divorce laws and the growing looseness of woman account for the fact that: first, every twelfth marriage ends in divorce; second, that since 1870 divorces have increased from 28 to 73 for every hundred thousand population; third, that adultery, since 1867, as ground for divorce, has increased 270.8 per cent.; fourth, that desertion increased 369.8 per cent.

Added to these startling figures is a vast amount of material, dramatic and literary, further elucidating this subject. Robert Herrick, in Together; Pinero, in Mid-Channel; Eugene Walter, in Paid in Full, and scores of other writers are discussing the barrenness, the monotony, the sordidness, the inadequacy of marriage as a factor for harmony and understanding.

The thoughtful social student will not content himself with the popular superficial excuse for this phenomenon. He will have to dig down deeper into the very life of the sexes to know why marriage proves so disastrous.

Edward Carpenter says that behind every marriage stands the life-long environment of the two sexes; an environment so different from each other that man and woman must remain strangers. Separated by an insurmountable wall of superstition, custom, and habit, marriage has not the potentiality of developing knowledge of, and respect for, each other, without which every union is doomed to failure.

Henrik Ibsen, the hater of all social shams, was probably the first to realize this great truth. Nora leaves her husband, not --- as the stupid critic would have it --- because she is tired of her responsibilities or feels the need of woman's rights, but because she has come to know that for eight years she had lived with a stranger and borne him children. Can there be any thing more humiliating, more degrading than a life-long proximity between two strangers? No need for the woman to know anything of the man, save his income. As to the knowledge of the woman---what is there to know except that she has a pleasing appearance? We have not yet outgrown the theologic myth that woman has no soul, that she is a mere appendix to man, made out of his rib just for the convenience of the gentleman who was so strong that he was afraid of his own shadow.

Perchance the poor quality of the material whence woman comes is responsible for her inferiority. At any rate, woman has no soul---what is there to know about her? Besides, the less soul a woman has the greater her asset as a wife, the more readily will she absorb herself in her husband. It is this slavish acquiescence to man's superiority that has kept the marriage institution seemingly intact for so long a period. Now that woman is coming into her own, now that she is actually growing aware of herself as a being outside of the master's grace, the sacred institution of marriage is gradually being undermined, and no amount of sentimental lamentation can stay it.

From infancy, almost, the average girl is told that marriage is her ultimate goal; therefore her training and education must be directed towards that end. Like the mute beast fattened for slaughter, she is prepared for that. Yet, strange to say, she is allowed to know much less about her function as wife and mother than the ordinary artisan of his trade. It is indecent and filthy for a respectable girl to know anything of the marital relation. Oh, for the inconsistency of respectability, that needs the marriage vow to turn something which is filthy into the purest and most sacred arrangement that none dare question or criticize. Yet that is exactly the attitude of the average upholder of marriage. The prospective wife and mother is kept in complete ignorance of her only asset in the competitive field---sex. Thus she enters into life-long relations with a man only to find herself shocked, repelled, outraged beyond measure by the most natural and healthy instinct, sex. It is safe to say that a large percentage of the unhappiness, misery, distress, and physical suffering of matrimony is due to the criminal ignorance in sex matters that is being extolled as a great virtue. Nor is it at all an exaggeration when I say that more than one home has been broken up because of this deplorable fact.

If, however, woman is free and big enough to learn the mystery of sex without the sanction of State or Church, she will stand condemned as utterly unfit to become the wife of a "good" man, his goodness consisting of an empty head and plenty of money. Can there be anything more outrageous than the idea that a healthy, grown woman, full of life and passion, must deny nature's demand, must subdue her most intense craving, undermine her health and break her spirit, must stunt her vision, abstain from the depth and glory of sex experience until a "good" man comes along to take her unto himself as a wife? That is precisely what marriage means. How can such an arrangement end except in failure? This is one, though not the least important, factor of marriage, which differentiates it from love.

Ours is a practical age. The time when Romeo and Juliet

risked the wrath of their fathers for love when Gretchen exposed herself to the gossip of her neighbors for love, is no more. If, on rare occasions young people allow themselves the luxury of romance they are taken in care by the elders, drilled and pounded until they become "sensible."

The moral lesson instilled in the girl is not whether the man has aroused her love, but rather is it, "How much?" The important and only God of practical American life: Can the man make a living? Can he support a wife? That is the only thing that justifies marriage. Gradually this saturates every thought of the girl; her dreams are not of moonlight and kisses, of laughter and tears; she dreams of shopping tours and bargain counters. This soul-poverty and sordidness are the elements inherent in the marriage institution. The State and the Church approve of no other ideal, simply because it is the one that necessitates the State and Church control of men and women.

Doubtless there are people who continue to consider love above dollars and cents.

Particularly is this true of that class whom economic necessity has forced to become self-supporting. The tremendous change in woman's position, wrought by that mighty factor, is indeed phenomenal when we reflect that it is but a short time since she has entered the industrial arena. Six million women wage-earners; six million women, who have the equal right with men to be exploited, to be robbed, to go on strike; aye, to starve even. Anything more, my lord? Yes, six million wage-workers in every walk of life, from the highest brain work to the most difficult menial labor in the mines and on the railroad tracks; yes, even detectives and policemen. Surely the emancipation is complete.

Yet with all that, but a very small number of the vast army of women wage-workers look upon work as a permanent issue, in the same light as does man. No matter how decrepit the latter, he has been taught to be independent, self-supporting. Oh, I know that no one is really independent in our economic tread mill; still, the poorest specimen of a man hates to be a parasite; to be known as such, at any rate.

The woman considers her position as worker transitory, to be thrown aside for the first bidder. That is why it is infinitely harder to organize women than men. "Why should I join a union? I am going to get married, to have a home." Has she not been taught from infancy to look upon that as her ultimate calling? She learns soon enough that the home, though not so large a prison as the factory, has more solid doors and bars. It has a keeper so faithful that naught can escape him. The most tragic part, however, is that the home no longer frees her from wage slavery; it only increases her task.

According to the latest statistics submitted before a Committee "on labor and wages, and congestion of Population," ten percent of the wage workers in New York City alone are married, yet they must continue to work at the most poorly paid labor in the world. Add to this horrible aspect the drudgery of house work, and what remains of the protection and glory of the home? As a matter of fact, even the middle class girl in marriage cannot speak of her home, since it is the man who creates her sphere. It is not important whether the husband is a brute or a darling. What I wish to prove is that marriage guarantees woman a home only by the grace of her husband. There she moves about in his home, year after year until her aspect of life and human affairs becomes as flat, narrow, and drab as her surroundings.

Small wonder if she becomes a nag, petty, quarrelsome, gossipy, unbearable, thus driving the man from the house. She could not go, if she wanted to; there is no place to go. Besides, a short period of married life, of complete surrender of all faculties, absolutely incapacitates the average woman for the outside world. She becomes reckless in appearance, clumsy in her movements, dependent in her decisions, cowardly in her judgment, a weight and a bore, which most men grow to hate and despise. Wonderfully inspiring atmosphere for the bearing of life, is it not?

But the child, how is it to be protected, if not for marriage? After all, is not that the most important consideration? The sham, the hypocrisy of it! Marriage protecting the child, yet thousands of children destitute and homeless. Marriage protecting the child, yet orphan asylums and reformatories over crowded, the Society for the Prevention of Cruelty to

Children keeping busy in rescuing the little victims from "loving" parents, to place them under more loving care, the Gerry Society. Oh, the mockery of it!

Marriage may have the power to "bring the horse to water," but has it ever made him drink? The law will place the father under arrest, and put him in convict's clothes; but has that ever stilled the hunger of the child? If the parent has no work, or if he hides his identity, what does marriage do then? It invokes the law to bring the man to "justice," to put him safely behind closed doors; his labor, however, goes not to the child, but to the State. The child receives but a blighted memory of its father's stripes.

As to the protection of the woman,---therein lies the curse of marriage. Not that it really protects her, but the very idea is so revolting, such an outrage and insult on life, so degrading to human dignity, as to forever condemn this parasitic institution.

It is like that other paternal arrangement --- capitalism. It robs man of his birthright, stunts his growth, poisons his body, keeps him in ignorance, in poverty and dependence, and then institutes charities that thrive on the last vestige of man's self-respect.

The institution of marriage makes a parasite of woman, an absolute dependent. It incapacitates her for life's struggle, annihilates her social consciousness, paralyzes her imagination, and then imposes its gracious protection, which is in reality a snare, a travesty on human character.

If motherhood is the highest fulfillment of woman's nature, what other protection does it need save love and freedom? Marriage but defiles, outrages, and corrupts her fulfillment. Does it not say to woman, Only when you follow me shall you bring forth life? Does it not condemn her to the block, does it not degrade and shame her if she refuses to buy her right to motherhood by selling herself? Does not marriage only sanction motherhood, even though conceived in hatred, in compulsion? Yet, if motherhood be of free choice, of love, of ecstasy, of defiant passion, does it not place a crown of thorns upon an innocent head and carve in letters of blood the hideous epithet, Bastard? Were marriage to contain all the virtues claimed for it, its crimes against motherhood would exclude it forever from the realm of love.

Love, the strongest and deepest element in all life, the harbinger of hope, of joy, of ecstasy; love, the defier of all laws, of all conventions; love, the freest, the most powerful molder of human destiny; how can such an all-compelling force be synonymous with that poor little State and Church-begotten weed, marriage?

Free love? As if love is anything but free! Man has bought brains, but all the millions in the world have failed to buy love. Man has subdued bodies, but all the power on earth has been unable to subdue love. Man has conquered whole nations, but all his armies could not conquer love. Man has chained and fettered the spirit, but he has been utterly helpless before love. High on a throne, with all the splendor and pomp his gold can command, man is yet poor and desolate, if love passes him by. And if it stays, the poorest hovel is radiant with warmth, with life and color. Thus love has the magic power to make of a beggar a king. Yes, love is free; it can dwell in no other atmosphere. In freedom it gives itself unreservedly, abundantly, completely.

All the laws on the statutes, all the courts in the universe, cannot tear it from the soil, once love has taken root. If, however, the soil is sterile, how can marriage make it bear fruit? It is like the last desperate struggle of fleeting life against death.

Love needs no protection; it is its own protection. So long as love begets life no child is deserted, or hungry, or famished for the want of affection. I know this to be true. I know women who became mothers in freedom by the men they loved. Few children in wedlock enjoy the care, the protection, the devotion free motherhood is capable of bestowing.

The defenders of authority dread the advent of a free motherhood, lest it will rob them of their prey. Who would fight wars? Who would create wealth? Who would make the policeman, the jailer, if woman were to refuse the indiscriminate breeding of children? The race, the race! shouts the king, the president, the capitalist, the priest. The race must be preserved, though woman be degraded to a mere machine, --- and the marriage institution is our only safety valve against the pernicious sex- awakening of woman. But in vain these frantic efforts to maintain a state of bondage. In vain, too, the edicts of the Church, the mad attacks of rulers, in vain even the arm of the law. Woman no longer wants to be a party to the production of a race of sickly, feeble, decrepit, wretched human beings, who have neither the strength nor moral courage to throw off the yoke of poverty and slavery. Instead she desires fewer and better children, begotten and reared in love and through free choice; not by compulsion, as marriage imposes. Our pseudo-moralists have yet to learn the deep sense of responsibility toward the child, that love in freedom has awakened in the breast of woman. Rather would she forego forever the glory of motherhood than bring forth life in an atmosphere that breathes only destruction and death. And if she does become a mother, it is to give to the child the deepest and best her being can yield. To grow with the child is her motto; she knows that in that manner alone call she help build true manhood and womanhood.

Ibsen must have had a vision of a free mother, when, with a master stroke, he portrayed Mrs. Alving. She was the ideal mother because she had outgrown marriage and all its horrors, because she had broken her chains, and set her spirit free to soar until it returned a personality, regenerated and strong. Alas, it was too late to rescue her life's joy, her

Oswald; but not too late to realize that love in freedom is the only condition of a beautiful life. Those who, like Mrs. Alving, have paid with blood and tears for their spiritual awakening, repudiate marriage as an imposition, a shallow, empty mockery. They know, whether love last but one brief span of time or for eternity, it is the only creative, inspiring, elevating basis for a new race, a new world.

In our present pygmy state love is indeed a stranger to most people. Misunderstood and shunned, it rarely takes root; or if it does, it soon withers and dies. Its delicate fiber cannot endure the stress and strain of the daily grind. Its soul is too complex to adjust itself to the slimy woof of our social fabric. It weeps and moans and suffers with those who have need of it, yet lack the capacity to rise to love's summit.

Someday, some day men and women will rise, they will reach the mountain peak, they will meet big and strong and free, ready to receive, to partake, and to bask in the golden rays of love. What fancy, what imagination, what poetic genius can foresee even approximately the potentialities of such a force in the life of men and women? If the world is ever to give birth to true companionship and oneness, not marriage, but love will be the parent.

A Conversation

When polyamory goes wrong, it can cause as much pain as the break-up of a monogamous relationship. The idea for this particular zine actually came out of a conversation that was highly critical of how our movement deals with polyamory. There is little discussion in general and what has been written errs too much on the evangelical side – life rarely that neat, and the same goes for our relationships.

What follows is a glimpse of some things that went wrong and lessons to be learned. An article would not do the subject justice so we have left it broken. We hope it shows that there is a responsibility by all partners in polyfidelity, and that we still have a long way to go

....experience of emotional and practical hierarchy. The other relationship was long established and committed. Throw into that issues of time and location... they were trying to get to where their prime partner was... ended up feeling like a mistress, there for mostly sexual relief. There was sexual comparison (a no, no really), lack of ability to feel my needs could ever be prioritised, lots of self-regulation and anger. Really hard to knowing when and if to ask for attention. General feeling of second bestness and low esteem (my problem I think)...

...That's so out of order. It also happens in monogamous

relationships with comparisons to an ex, of course, but that is not quite the same....

... Ended up either not being able to deal with the deep stu-ff at all or me going to pieces all the time because we can't get enough time/space together to actually work through it. The fear that if I start asking for what I know I need I'll end up with nothing, because they are just not in a position to provide it...

...I was not self-assertive enough and really should have got out. I had one other relationship in that time which was much better but didn't work out. It would all have been better if we both had primary relationships rather than me being a secondary to them and me not having anyone else. This is the key point about what went wrong. I had nowhere else to go at that time really and he could offer very little. This feels like being fed scraps when you are starving...

... I also beat myself up a lot for not being 'cool' enough to cope with non-monogamy but now on reflection it was all a bit nasty and power was too much with him.

...Trying to be cool in relationships sounds like a recipe for misery. Actually I know it is. Difficult habit to break though.

... I never really knew what he had been doing and who with...

and total breakdown in trust and communication because I did not have the courage to ask or the ability to cope when they told me. General feeling of physical vulnerability…

… it was a bad relationship and the secondary polyamory aspect just added to it…

… Experiences of secondary relationships are precisely the point – the existence of secondary, or partial, relationships is one of the basic differences between monogamy and polyamory. If only the partner who matters is the primary one, everyone else is a bit on the side, a concept monogamy has no problem with, but is pretty grim if you are the 'bit'…

…A relationship which has been going on for years is simply MORE than one that is just started. Especially where the older one involves living together. I do not see how any negotiation that goes on can possibly be seen as equal. For me it's been either 'this one isn't really negotiable – you have to fit around it, or an increasingly nasty realization that the other partner doesn't want to be in this situation, our joint lover is dealing with things rather badly, and I'm getting caught up in their relationship's problems… I have felt partly responsible for that other relationship, especially in the cases where I already knew them as a friend before I started seeing their partner. BUT the first case doesn't necessarily mean there isn't room for something good…

… Although knowing that, given who/what/how we are,

could only be a 'partial' relationship - we'd never be 'madly in love and want to live together forever' – not going into the deep messy stuff, or even the everyday needs, has been much easier…

… Also the knowledge, not unique to polyamorous relationships, that passion sometimes thrives on a certain amount of distance – it is possible to know someone too much and maybe I'm avoiding that.

…Being told that they did not have room in their life for more partners and I was last on the list. That was fucking grim. Honest on their part but how am I supposed to react?...

…This is critical I think. So much writing on polyamory seems to be based on people who are in a primary relationship and want to broaden their horizons, or on people who don't want to be dependent on one primary but keep several equals, and if those are the only perspectives then it's fucking self-centred – the negative positions we have been in exists, a lot…

…You CAN'T always have what you want, there aren't enough lovers to go around, no-one does polyamory perfectly, very few even do it well, and people are going to get hurt. Secondary partners probably worse than most. This isn't a dismissal of the concept, but it's something people need to face up to more…

...And it's political – we're talking about inequality and privilege.

...but I do not feel like my views are representative. I am pretty sure I will be accused of being stuck in a monogamous mindset, which I am happy to admit I often am...

...Your views are representative of you. Monogamy suites some situation, some people. Anyone who tells you monogamy is wrong is as bigoted as someone who tells you it is compulsory...

...I think what we're coming to here is about about people and situations – the sort of polyamory most writers on the subject seem to promote probably can work pretty well, or at least equally, in situations where everyone has a grounded space in roughly the type of relationships they want. However, while love may not be a finite quality, time, energy, physical circumstances, etc are, and in real situations there often just isn't enough of a particular person to go round. Scarcity, in other words, to be cynically economic about it. It's going to hurt. Sometimes it's going to hurt too much to be worth doing...

... And some people are less suited to deal with the chaos and negotiation aspects than others – particularly those of us who classify as control freaks. Or those of us with self-esteem or martyrdom issues, who start from a position that we should attempt to take the pain of the situation onto ourselves, even when it's not our fault. Or those of us (the majority in my experience) who have trouble communicating their feelings…

Anarchy is love, Love is anarchy
Anarchist loving – many choices

Like many I didn't become anarchistic after reading a book on it. It was something that I felt my way towards before I had a name for it from the many moments of questioning why things had to be done in a specific way, feeling uncomfortable with "unfair" situations of power and seeking a supportive community. When I did read a book on anarchism I recognised the principles of mutual aid, non-hierarchy and self management as how I was trying to live my life.

These principles are integral to my approach to most of my relationships. There isn't one way to do friendship or love. Friendship and love can't healthily be about dependence or isolation. I think it is important to identify and challenge the power dynamics in my relationships. I don't believe in certainty or forever but I do believe in commitment (to try and make a relationship work rather then to stay in it regardless), honesty and trust. Any relationship needs constant renegotiation, we all change with time and circumstances and sometimes this means the end of a relationship or a significant change in how it works.

I have never had wedding fantasies. I don't long to live as a 2.4 nuclear family. Rather than ask me what I do want from a relationship people often just see as it a choice between monogamy and polyamory and fill in the answer from this narrow range of options. I don't see myself as either and believe that really the choices are infinite and fortunately without labels.

I can choose who I love, how I love them, how many people I love and this can change with time both for me as an individual or me in a particular relationship. I currently only have one "lover" (which is the right choice right now for us taking into accounts our needs and one that we have consciously made). But this is not the only person that I love or have an intense and deep relationship with and I don't feel that I have to choose to love only one person. Although clearly I chosen to have a very clear boundary between one of my relationships and all the others. I like to think I make a choice to make the relationship with my lover one that seeks to draw other people around us to be part of our lives.

Relationships with people with different boundaries can be testing. I have certainly found myself in uncomfortable situations with friends who draw their boundaries in a different place. This is a challenge but surely one where the situation is about mutual respect of our different takes on where those boundaries lie. At time unfortunately it can feel like a judgement on a choice not to be polyamourous (and implicitly that not being radical enough).

Polyamory clearly works for lots of people but it isn't the right answer for everyone all of the time. I think the priority of a relationship is that it works for those within it, without any fucked up power dynamics and without isolating them from the rest of the world. The rest of how people want their relationship to be is a lot more complex then just a choice between monogamy and polyamory, an opportunity of infinite exciting ways to be and do things.

Love and let love...............................

8 Points on Relationship Anarchy

Andie Nordgren (translation by Leo Nordwall and Elli Åhlvik)

You can love a lot of people - each relationship is unique

Relationship Anarchy (RA) questions the idea that love is a special, limited feeling which is real only when kept between two people at any given moment. It is possible to love more than one person - your relationship to one doesn't diminish your relationships to the others. Don't value and compare – appreciate each other! No one needs to be highlighted as a partner to make a relationship "real". Every relationship stands on its own, a meeting between independent equals.

Love and Respect is to have no demands

Refraining from demands as a basis of a relationship is to show respect towards other people's independency and capability of making decisions on their own. You having feelings for others or a history together doesn't give you the right to set rules or make demands. Try instead to explore how you can develop a relationship without disregarding each other's essential values and opinions. Rather than compromising in every situation, make it possible to make different choices without letting that cause a crisis in the relationship. Demandlessness is the only way to be completely sure that everyone in a relationship is there of their own free will. It's not "real love" to adjust to each other according to an existing template.

Give yourself a solid point of view

How do you want others to treat you? And I mean everyone. What are your premises and how do you define your boundaries? What kind of people do you want to have around and how do you want your relationships to be? Find such a core point of view and work with all your relationships according to it. Don't make any exception to the rules or 'special cases' for different people to prove that you really care for someone specific.

Remember the heterosexual norm but don't be afraid

Remember that there is an incredibly powerful set of normative beliefs telling you how life and real love should be. People will wonder and question your relationships. Talk with loved ones to find escapes and tricks to avoid norms and rules that cause problems. But remember to create positive alternatives and fight for something, not just against the norm. Don't allow your relationships to be driven by fear of societal norms.

Spontaneity instead of duty

To be able to be spontaneous – to act without the fear of being punished and without obligations – is what makes radical relationships come to life. Spontaneity is above all else the opposite to duty. You would want a relationship where you spend time with each other just because you want to, not out of a sense of duty. Spontaneity is not about never planning ahead or thinking before acting, it's about building relationships without duties and demands. Organize your relationships in a way so that they enable spontaneousness!

Fake it 'til you make it

Sometimes it might sound like you have to be some kind of übermensch to "stand life" as a relationship anarchist. It's not true. Try using the trick "fake it 'til you make it", which means that you imagine how you would have done in various difficult situations if you were as strong and cool as you'd like. Make these thoughts simple guidelines you use in situations where you feel too weak. Talk to other people about how they handle things and never blame yourself!

Trust is better than being suspicious

Assume that everyone near you wants you to be happy. The common idea that egoism is the sole power driving human behaviour is bullshit. You and others around you want to acknowledge and communicate with each other but sometimes there is so much to be dealt with in life that you don't have the energy to take care of anyone but yourself. The better the relationships and environments you can create for yourself and others, the more time and energy you can spend on others and acknowledge one another. Give people lots of opportunities to discuss with, explain, care for you and take responsibility for the relationship but remember to take care of yourself. Remember your personal boundaries.

Change through communication

Whenever people do something together there is a norm on how to act and what to do – a norm on how a the situation should turn out. If you and people around you won't talk about the whats, hows and whys, everything will turn out as the norm dictates. Communication, common action and a will to change is the only way to break free from the norms. Radical relationships must have open discussions as their main component, not as a state of emergency. Remember that trust is your most important tool. We are so used to people never quite saying what they actually mean, that we have to search for and try to interpret what they're really after. These assumptions are always based on societal norms or your previous expericnces, which isn't necessarily true in your relationship. Talk to each other!

First published at;

*http://www.polyamory.org.uk/relationship_anarchy.htm*l

The Rise of Polyamory:
Leftist men's self-serving cure-all for sexism

"lost clown"

> "The pornographic conception of female power is fundamental to the anti-feminism of sexual-liberation movements in which unlimited sexual use of women by men is defined as freedom for both: she wants it; he responds: Voila! The revolution."
>
> *Andrea Dworkin, Right Wing Women*

Poly; more than one, many, multi-

Amorous; loving, having to do with love, inclined to love, in love.

I believe in polyamory, but only in a society where everyone is equal, where everyone is allowed to be human. Polyamory, therefore, cannot exist in our society.

I have been a polyamorist all my life, before I had knowledge of the word polyamory. I am still a polyamorist today, but I cannot bring myself to practice anymore, because polyamory as a mutually fulfilling practice cannot exist in a society that does not see me as human. The rise of polyamory as the preferred lifestyle in the radical leftist/

anarchist circles parallels the "sexual revolution" of the late '60s movement. This supposed sexual freedom for women is done not for our benefit, but for the benefit of men. The ultimate goal for these "radical" men is still the fuck.

In both the present and 60s "sexual revolutions" women's sexuality has not been freed. It is not our sexuality that we are "reclaiming," but the sexuality that men desire us to have because it benefits them. Being open to the fuck, as all polyamorous women are supposed to be, is men's definition of liberated female sexuality. There has not been a women orientated sexual revolution yet. There needs to be. Having multiple partners at any given time is not liberating for women, for we are not seen as human, but as sexual chattel. We are passed back and forth between brothers in arms; our sexuality defined not by ourselves, but by those same men. One thing almost all leftist men, our supposed allies, agree upon is that polyamory is freeing for women. This is cause for examination. Are these men our allies? What constitutes an ally? In the case of sexism an ally is a man who sees women as human beings. Allies are men who jeopardize their privileged status with other men by defending women. This also means (but is not limited to) being willing to be arrested and/or beaten (as the police are liable to do these days) at an action or protest in support of or for women's rights. The men who purport to be our allies may support polyamory, but only a few have actually laid their bodies on the line, the way my sisters and I do daily, for women's issues. Unless they are willing to jeopardize their status with other men and put their bodies on the line they are not allies, and should be treated as enemies.

Polyamory, in essence, is based upon a respect for all people involved, and respect is impossible without equality. Polyamory is taught as a way for women to reclaim their sexuality, but we cannot reclaim things that have always been defined for us by other people: namely men. Men have defined our sexuality; they have defined words used to describe women's sexuality and behaviors such as bitch, slut, whore, cunt, etc. Where are the positive words to define women's sexuality? The lack of their existence is proof that women have never defined our own sexuality. When we attempt to "reclaim" these words, and give them a new meaning they remain hurtful to us, as they retain their original meanings and are still used negatively by others. An example: the American Heritage Dictionary defines the term bitch as "a female canine animal, esp. a dog" and "a spiteful or overbearing woman." I am neither, and no matter how positively I use the term it will always mean a female dog and a spiteful woman. As long as we continue to use the words and behaviors defined by the oppressors we will never break the cycle of oppression; we will never truly be free. Female sexuality can never be reclaimed; it must be defined in the first place, something that has never happened. Reclamation is misleading, and an ultimate dead end. We can never reclaim anything that was never ours in the first place. Reclamation of our bodies, and of terms used to describe us is not a good strategy, or even possible. The terms of "liberated" female sexuality have not been defined by women, but by men to their own benefit.

The "sexual revolution" of the '60s was supported by leftist men. Women had legitimate reason to say no, because of a real fear of pregnancy, so leftist men started backing legal abortion. When abortion was legalized, and women continued saying no, because of the real problem that they were being treated as sexual chattel, leftist men abandoned the abortion issue. Some even argued against legalized abortion. Why? Because safe, legal abortion was supposed to ensure men's sexual access to any woman. Now during the second Amerikan "sexual revolution," abortion rights are under attack, birth control is more accessible[1], and safe sex is a popular catch phrase. Yet nothing has changed. Women have more control over and access to knowledge of our reproductive organs, but that makes men believe that they should have unlimited sexual access to women. Our male counterparts on the radical left gloss over feminist issues of human equality, and substitute the self-serving cure-all of polyamory. To them being polyamorous means that they are supporting women, however this is not the case. They are unwilling to acknowledge their privilege as men or their behaviors that reinforce sexism in society and they still expect us to be available for a quick fuck; something that is fulfilling for them alone.

Both of these so-called revolutions have produced the

1.Washington State Department of Social and Health Services in conjunction with Planned Parenthood is currently offering the Take Charge Plan in which free annual exams and birth control is offered to low income women and men. This program will last until at least 2005 as it is a pilot program. It is open to ALL Washington State residents, regardless of age.

mother/child dynamic absent of accessible fathers. If the move towards polyamory is supposed to be liberating, why then does it create the same absentee fathers, and alienated mother/child pairs? Where is the day care or the support for mothers within the revolutionary movements? Why is revolution inaccessible to them? We have long passed the days when women gained access to and were allowed to remain in movement groups only because they were being fucked by one of the male members. (Women were only included in groups while being fucked. When the men tired of them the radical group dropped them.) These days, women can work in radical leftist groups without having to sleep with anyone in them to begin with, though human equality still has not been achieved. Women are not asked to join groups because of what they can offer the group through ideas or work, but instead they are only allowed to join to enhance and fill the dating pool. Under the new definition of "sexual liberation," i.e. polyamory, women do not gain access to the group by one man, but they gain access to the group by being polyamorous; by being accessible to all the men of the group. Once women join these groups they are treated like fresh "meat" and aggressively pursued. An activist man once told me that the main reason men became activists was to get laid. I could not believe him at the time, thinking that people became activists because they couldn't bear to allow injustices to continue, but the actions of these "activist" men have proven his statement to be true. I have seen men aggressively pursue new women in these groups until the women finally give in and sleep with the overly aggressive men. They are then used, discarded, and disappear from the group entirely because the problems with these men are dismissed as personal problems, not a problem the group has with allowing and enabling these men to abuse women and perpetuate misogynistic behaviors. All this has been done in the name of "polyamory."

I have time and again defended polyamory by saying that most people do not practice it correctly. There is a lack of the respect and honesty that is inherent in equality, and I loathe the way people use the term polyamory to describe their relationships when it is obviously structured around free sexual access for men, not reciprocity and self-determination for both. A true sexual revolution would require the men in these groups to study and admit their privilege. The true sexual revolution will have men viewing us as equal, as human not pornography, and will be based on mutuality and respect. There can be no sexual freedom without economic and political freedom. As long as men have power over women in any aspect of our society women will not be free sexually, because our sexual freedom is dependent upon whether or not we are valued as human. Men do not study their privilege; it is unimportant to them if women leave different groups, because the man, by nature of his manhood, was obviously doing more work then she was, because he is human, and she is not. In most instances the women work harder (we have to in order for our work to even be slightly acknowledged), but as we see daily, women's work has no real worth to men unless it is sexual in nature when it is encouraged. In a true sexual revolution real women's work (not the work historically assigned to us) would be valued as much as the men's work and these men would not be allowed to continue chasing women away from activist groups.

Men argue that polyamory is freeing for women; it releases us from the old idea of ownership. This is not true. Under the new polyamorous definition of female sexuality women are not owned by one man, instead we are owned by many. In our new "sexual freedom," we are a fuck all can enjoy instead of just one. When we decide we aren't polyamorous, given the male defined terms and standards, we are called "old-fashioned" a term that by leftist standards is degrading and humiliating. Radical women do not like being equated with old-fashioned ideas of sexuality, which are laden with inequalities. We are trying to claim our minds, our hearts, and our bodies, and we are also struggling not to be perceived as wanting a home and family. In fact this is not what we want at all. We want relationships in which we are viewed as equals, as humans, and if a family results from that it may be good, but it's not what we're looking for. Because of the views towards non-polyamorous relationships I have seen many unwilling women sleep with other men in order to prove that they are not "old-fashioned," but that they are in fact new, "liberated" women.

Prostitution for male attention and approval is a common theme, no matter how radical we are. As long as we value our 'partners" wants and desires above our own needs we will continue to prostitute ourselves. We need to take the power away from men to coerce us using our so-called liberated sexuality. This is only one of many coercion tactics that men use on us, but it raises a very important question: why do we need to be coerced into liberty? If these types of polyamorous relationships were actually liberating why do women need to be coerced into them? Liberation does not require underhanded tactics that leftist men use such as shaming and name-calling. This is not a free choice for many women, and cannot be seen as liberty.

When we decide not to share our beds and our bodies with more than one man we risk being called anti-sexual. Many women I know who choose this path are not anti-sexual, but anti-sexism. They choose to form their own ideas about their sexuality, instead of blindly following a sexual doctrine that they do not find fulfilling. This is the true meaning of sexual liberation. The freedom to say yes or no. The smear campaign against women who say no raises serious questions about whose sexuality is being freed. If we happen to be heterosexual, we choose to wait for someone that we consider an ally who is worthy of having a relationship with us, and these men are hard to find. When our definition of female sexuality is not men's definition of female sexuality we are pressured to conform, and if we don't we are shunned, ridiculed, attacked, and humiliated. If we choose to have a relationship with one man, who we consider to be our ally, we are defined as old-fashioned, or sometimes we are seen as women who have not yet liberated our sexuality. A committed relationship with one man ensures that we will be able to hold him accountable in ways that would be impossible with many men. So why are women who participate in polyamory the only ones who are seen as free and liberated? Isn't the ability to choose true liberation?

I no longer support polyamorous relationships in public, because so many people, mostly men, are wanton and harmful in their practice of it. That, unfortunately but logically, is the norm not to the exception. In a society of true equals, where women are allowed to be human, polyamory is a wonderful choice. Some of us are capable of loving many people at the same time, and want to be able to have relationships with all of them, but love is not the basis for the current polyamorous relationship, the fuck is.

Radical leftist/anarchist circles are just reconstructions of larger society. They purport to be fighting against capitalism and all its effects, but never once attack the major ways in which capitalism survives, i.e. sexism, racism, classism, heterosexism, etc. Capitalism is inherently hierarchical. In order for it to prosper there must be a higher class, which reaps its rewards (money, power), and a lower class that labors for very little pay and supports the higher class, thereby allowing its existence. They do not address the class divisions or the ways in which sexism segregates women into the lower classes, because as men, they are not affected by it. Women are trapped in low paying lower class work and unpaid household labor. Raising a family, cooking, and cleaning remain unpaid labors that fall into the category of "women's work," but if you were to clean someone else's house, cook someone else's dinner, and watch someone else's kids you would be paid at least minimum wage. Doing these things for people in your immediate family and your own house are expected of women. In today's society women, especially women of color and single mothers are the poorest in the nation. It has been that way for too long. Society as we know it was born off the unpaid labor of women and people of color. Amerika was built off our backs, with our tears and our blood. There will be no revolution without the destruction of the white male supremist power structure. As long as one group is defined as normal (white straight middle-class men), and another group is defined as other (women, people of color, homosexuals) there will be no free society. These very oppressive structures are mirrored in the radical groups of today, thereby making it so that there will never truly be the much needed fundamental change.

"We'll deal with [sexism] after the revolution." This is an actual statement that was once made to me, but it has also been communicated in much subtler ways. As mentioned before, when men in activist groups who abuse and eventually chase women away from the groups are allowed to remain we are in effect saying that women are unimportant. Our cause is more important than the rampant misogyny in our ranks. We are too busy to deal with you, because you, woman, are not important. We, men, decide what is important, because we, men, are human. You are not. Women in these groups are always asking why there are so few people of color in them. The men pay this some lip service, but ultimately do nothing. They seem to think that if the question is posed then they are effectively working on diversity. It's acceptable to be openly sexist, but it is taboo to seem racist. No question is asked about the lack of women, however. It is simply not a matter of diversity if there are few to no women; it simply becomes a group that women do not want to join. The men in these groups have many different reasons why they think women do not want to join; sexism is not one of them. No one cares why women do not want to join, or why they leave one after the other. They have many excuses for why women do not want to join these groups that are based on the sexist beliefs in women's inferiority. Some of these beliefs include the fact that activism is confrontational; it is risky, intense, and laden with pressure. Women are not able to be confrontational or be strong enough to participate in these groups in the long run, since we are weaker and have been taught to avoid confrontation and to be nice. Another argument that may be seen is that women don't fully comprehend the issues, rather we are stupid and superficial, and cannot see how vital the issues are to our fight. These blatantly sexist thoughts about women are ingrained into our society, and the people who are trying to change our society don't seem to feel like these issues need to be changed. In the cases I have mentioned of the predatory sexist men, the group thinks that when the woman leaves it was because she was being oversensitive. What happened in reality is that she was being treated as subhuman, got fed up, tried to stand up for herself, get support from the radical group, and was ignored or attacked. No one would listen to her. No one would help her. Those were personal issues between her and the man. They are never seen as group issues; even when the same scenario is played out over and over with the same man and different women.

In various leftist/anarchist groups women are welcomed, but it becomes apparent right away that they are not welcomed for their ideas, plans, and actions. When they have a good idea it is usually overlooked until a man stands up and says the exact same thing, which is when it becomes a brilliant idea. In many instances the men don't even wait long to re-present the woman's idea as their own. It usually occurs less then five minutes after the woman originally presented the idea. This is not the only time when our voices and actions are ignored; when women put their bodies on the line at various protests or actions their voices are not only ignored by the media, but silenced by the all too eager self elected male spokesman who feels justified, because he believes that he has all knowledge and authority about whatever campaign they are working on. He feels that men, especially himself, are the natural leaders of such groups, being more knowledgeable, and therefore should be the ones speaking to the public. With all of the egotism, male self-aggrandizement, and sexism, it is not surprising that the absence of women in these groups goes on unnoticed; our contributions go by unacknowledged. Radical women should stand up and fight this. We should not stand aside while our voices are silenced. In the leftist/anarchist scope equality is certainly spoken about, but the actions by these groups continue to prove that women are still valued less than men. Or, as commonly seen in greater society, we are valued for our sex, not our voices.

It is not surprising, therefore, that both the first and second waves of Amerikan feminism have been born out of social activist movements. The first, the women's suffrage movement, was born out of the abolitionist movement. When women realized that their voices were not being heard, because they were female voices, and that the fight to free the slaves and give them rights only in actuality meant freedom and rights for black men, not women, they got fed up and organized. They realized that political and social equality was a much larger issue then abolition alone. These women still continued to fight in the abolitionist movement because they understood that gaining freedom and rights for the slaves was integral to gaining their freedom as women. The second wave occurred after the Civil Rights movement, where women were assigned such menial, sex-specific tasks as fetching coffee, filing, and answering phones. They were glorified unpaid secretaries. Soon after came the anti-Vietnam War movement in which women's roles were likewise segregated, but during the anti-war movement they were also faced with the so- called revolution in which they were expected to make themselves sexually available for the men they were working alongside. A good example of this is the anti-war propaganda poster that says "Girls say yes to boys who say no." Before the mass realization of the left's exploitation of women's bodies, the second wave, women were only included in organizations for their sex. A similar consciousness raising is necessary now. We need to realize what women in the '70s realized: Men only value us for our sex and historically defined women's work. Women prove daily, and especially in large-scale social movements, that we will put other people's rights and needs above our own. It's sad to think that all these brilliant women were abused for years before they stood up and fought, and after all their hard work the same patterns are being repeated today. No longer should this be the case. We should be organizing now, in every group we work in, everyday of our lives. It is time for us to stop putting our basic right to be human aside. It is time we think about ourselves and about ending all oppression. We have surely waited long enough for this.

One cannot wait for things to get better; we can't wait for revolution. People must struggle and organize. Women have been struggling for centuries, and we should not have to struggle anymore. We need to organize ourselves across the lines of race, age, religion, class, and country. We need to include transgender and intersex women. We all fall victim to the same oppression.

Today, Amerikan feminism is dominant. White, liberal, middle-class Amerikan feminism has become the standard by which Amerikan women judge all other forms of feminism. Liberal feminism is predominant in this country, because it has been made very accessible through organizations like the national chapter of NOW and publications like Ms. It is how we distinguish between "feminists" and "radical feminists." The American Heritage Dictionary defines the term radical as "one who advocates fundamental or revolutionary change." Radical feminists are women who advocate not compromising for anything short of basic human rights now. We want a fundamental change of the systems of power that control our world; we do not want small changes. We are not satisfied with small gains within the hierarchical system; we want the whole damn pie thrown out and a new one made. The revolution needs to be radicalized. We understand that other people's freedom is integral to our own. We are the women who will not compromise; we are the women who take feminism "too far." We are the women who will not settle until hierarchy is dismantled, and our words reflect that. The mainstream liberal groups may reach many women, but it is our job to then radicalize these women. Liberal women's fight is closely related to radical women's, as the loss of any rights we have gained in the past 90 years affects liberals as acutely as it affects radicals. Take for instance our reproductive rights. Both liberals and radicals fought for reproductive rights, and both would be hurt equally with the sudden loss of autonomy over our bodies. Even if we do not agree on everything, radical and liberal women need each other, and need to work together to abolish sexism. One of the problems faced by radical women, is that most people's conception of radical feminism is that our thoughts and words are harsh, but they are in fact nothing short of the truth and should not be coopted. Many radical feminists are not radical at all. We ask for complete equality, and some people are not comfortable with this because it means an overhaul of everything in society as it now stands.

Capitalism and hierarchy, the means by which our society is run, are integral to our continued oppression, and one of the things that we have become accustomed to today. Fighting against those two fundamentals of society that we take for granted as normal is a large change, as it is the only version of society that we have ever known. It can be intimidating to fight against something that is so familiar to us. If we are committed to a society in which all people, including women, are equal, then we must push ourselves to work towards our goals, especially when we have to push our boundaries of comfort. We cannot allow our personal prejudices or our fear of change to interfere with our struggle. The changes we need to make are radical and may make some people uncomfortable at the beginning, but they are necessary to our freedom.

It is imperative that we listen to women who have different backgrounds than us, and hear what they're saying in order to be able to work with women from all over.

We must be willing to learn from women who face multiple forms of oppression, and who come from different countries and experience different forms of oppression than we do. This is part of acknowledging the dominance of Amerikan feminism. Those of us who are white have much to learn from those of us who aren't. We must address our own personal racism, classism, heterosexism, transphobia, etc., in order to work with all women. Amerikan feminists, especially white ones, have privilege in relation to women from poorer countries. Those of us who do not know that ending all forms of oppression is the only way by which we will gain freedom as women need to learn this fact. Each form of oppression depends upon other forms of oppression to continue to work. It is impossible to get rid of one without the other. As long as hierarchy exists so will oppression. We must come to the table with open hearts and open minds, because no matter what our differences we share a common bond as women. We are oppressed as women and must unite as women, because if we leave any woman behind we will not get rid of sexism and patriarchy. Every woman must be free or else sexism will still exist, and our goal is for all women to be treated as human. If we discriminate because of someone's race, religion, etc. we will imitate the behaviors of our oppressors. This does not give us freedom; it gives us more hierarchy and more oppression.

We cannot repeat the patterns of hierarchy and dominance in our society, or else things will never change. The so□called radical groups that do not address sexism are repeating these patterns. They perpetuate and encourage male dominance over women, and are not truly radical groups. They enforce hierarchy and dominance and then deny that they are doing so. We must NOT repeat this among ourselves. In working with many different women we must set an example of a truly nonhierarchical group. To do this we all must embrace other women's ways of coping with oppression. What do any of us know to make us believe that our ways are the one true way with which to fight patriarchy? We cannot hold others up to our ideals of what feminism is. The ideal is the basic right to be human. Period. We cannot expect everyone to fight in the same manner, and we cannot exclude people because our attitudes and beliefs differ from theirs.

We are all fighting the same fight, and if we don't include all women we will never see freedom, period. We are human. That's our fight.

Women of all different backgrounds need to value our lives first. We need to stand up to this pattern of being valued for our bodies. By working in these sexist groups, we are not putting ourselves on the line in order to create a society any fairer to us than the one we already exist in. The patterns of polyamory in supposedly radical groups are evidence of how we are valued by the movement; we are still around to be fucked. We must raise our voices in opposition to this. We are worth more.

Radical sisters, we must learn that if men are not willing to make a stand for our basic right to be human, if they are not willing to put their bodies on the line as we do everyday for our basic right to autonomy, then they are not our allies in revolution. They DO NOT want to jeopardize their roles as the privileged gender class in our society. They DO NOT want to see us as human. This is something we must learn and remember no matter how radical the group in which we work, no matter what the nature of the campaign, or our beliefs. We must value ourselves at least as much as the causes we are working for, and understand that these campaigns will never succeed unless they take women's issues into account. We must fight. This is a hard concept for women to learn and practice. We have been taught all our lives to value others before ourselves. Our mothers valued their children before themselves. Sometimes they valued their husbands and their "acceptable" family lives above themselves. In the cases of revolutionary women they valued abolition first, Civil Rights for African-American men first, ending the Vietnam War first, themselves last. We seem doomed to continue repeating this pattern. Enough is enough. We must organize within organizations. We must not let these men, whom we absurdly believe to be our allies in struggle contrary to their actions and our experiences, continue to value us purely for sex. We must define our own terms and forge our own path. We are activists; it is time we fought for ourselves.

First published in Off Our Backs (www.offourbacks.org) and available in full length form at;

http://angryforareason.blogspot.com/2006/05/long-awaited-polyamory-and-activism.html,

A Green Anarchist Project on Freedom and Love

mae bee

This piece is not advocating another option, another "choice" of relating for couples. It is rather a recognition that our "common project" - the abolition of all power relations – includes the abolition of coercive/closed relationships. these are those relationships with fixed stature, those relationships with rules or permanent contracts. these relationships cannot really be part of a free society. and just as with other coercive relations at odds with our freedom they must be confronted by all who seek such freedom and communities.

> *" We need to pursue our sexual encounters as we do all of our relationships, in total opposition to this society, not out of any sense of revolutionary duty, but because it is the only way possible to have full, rich uninhibited sexual relations in which loveceases to be a desperate mutual dependence and instead becomes an expansive exploration of the unknown."*
> *(On sexual poverty – wilful disobedience 4)*

> *" At best then, anarcho-primitivism is a convenient label used to characterise diverse individuals with a common project: the abolition of all power relations. E.g structures of control, coercion, domination and*

exploitation – and the creation of a form of community that excludes such relations."
(John Moore – An introduction to Anarcho-Primitivism)

RULES OF ENGAGEMENT

i am going to use the term "rule relationships" or sometimes "coercive or restricted relationships" because i do not know another generic term for monogamous relationships and those which claim to be polyamorous or open but have rules. by the latter i mean those where the consenting coercion is that whilst a loved one is not restricted to one person only but they are still not at liberty or encouraged to follow their desires.

from a political view these two relationship options are the same. if your reasons for non-monogamy are merely about increased sexual gratification with an increased number of people then rule relationships may serve that purpose. if, however, it is through the desire to create communities not couples, for desire not consent, for trust not fear. why then, the "banned list", the "not in my company", the regulations must all go. when open relationships or free relationships are referred to in this text i mean exactly that..

PERSONAL NOTE: whilst this short piece hopes to inspire thoughts it is not meant to be complete: much is missing from it.. And if it causes controversy I hope that is to arouse emotions, discussion and hopefully other writings, rather than cause upset.. It is merely my current contribution to something ongoing rather than a final word.

CHOICE AND RESPECT

whilst there is an acceptance of open relationships within our eco-anarchist communities, there is equal acceptance of restricted relationships. this comes in part from sound motives: people can be at liberty to agree their own relationships, there are no set patterns, etc. however, there are a host of reasons why this libertarian outlook is an idle one.

firstly, in mass societies we consent to all sorts of coercive relationships. working for a wage, signing on, being a customer and therefore an exploiter of workers.,,,,,indeed it is difficult to find many relations which are not based on some degree of coercion or exploitation. consenting to coercive relations in no way indicates that we desire them. since the 1970's (at least!) radical feminism has been exploring the very major differences between consent and desire, particularly in the realm of love and sex. many women consent to sex to avoid rape, for example. consent is rooted in the language of law and of property rights. this is why it is useful for mass societies but useless for creating radical ones. it is certainly not a radical place in which to understand a world based on desire. and surely, our sexual relationships are one of the more obvious places to situate desire and not consent.

so, people consent to rule relationships as they do to other coercive relations but do they desire them? fundamentally, this is an oxymoron. we do not need to make rules about things we do not fear. if two people only desired to have sexual relations with each other then there would not need to be rules made to govern this. this does not make it a coercive relationship, although it makes it literal monogamy. the coercion is in the governing of that desire, not just for oneself but for the one you desire and love.

monogamy is a contract precisely because we do not expect literal monogamy, because we expect our lover to desire sex with others who are not us. maybe not now, but certainly in the future. we also expect our lover to make rules to govern our desire because we have no trust in the singleness of our sexual desire either. it is ridiculous then, for monogamists to claim they have forbidden each other to have sex with others because they only desire sex with each other.

rule relationships then operate on sexual consent but not desire. although of course, there are reasons we do desire to coerce and be coerced. we desire this because we desire to control, own and possess that which is around us. this is a desire fixed in the myth that we can do this with living beings, and worse, that we can do this in the name of love when really it is only control. if we cannot give up our belief in possession of the limitless: and by that i mean things like love, affection, sexual desire......how do we begin to relinquish control of that which is limited: such as the resources of the world? an inability, or rather a lack of desire, to free the ones we love the most – and at no real cost to ourselves – suggests we are so far gone in the madness of mass society that there is no going forward, no coming home to freedom.

it is worth mentioning here, although only as an incidental aside, that outside of using constant surveillance and/or force, nobody can really stop their loved one loving or fucking another. they can only choose to believe they can which to me would suggest a form of mental illness.

JEALOUSY AND OTHER FEELINGS

the infant often reacts to a new sibling at it's mothers body with extreme jealousy, intense feelings of rivalry and anger, and ultimately ownership. as adults we watch with sympathy but not horror. we do not expect the mother to put the newcomer away or keep her love for the new one out of the older child's eyeshot. we expect instead that the mother will reassure the first child she still loves and cares for it as well as assuring the child she loves and cares for the new baby also. except in very rare cases the child's jealousy lessens and the child accepts the situation.

in comparison we have the relationship of adults:

the adult often reacts to a new person at it's lover's body with extreme jealousy, intense feelings of rivalry and anger, and ultimately ownership. as adults we expect either the newcomer to be put away (monogamy) or for a code of conduct to be obeyed, such as love for the new one to be out of the first one's eyeshot (restrictive relationships). of all the complex and different emotions between the three, or more, people, we give the jealousy and rivalry of the first lover priority.

how can this possibly happen? this seems to demonstrate a civilised and artificial separation of the potentials of children and of adults. we deem children's emotions unreasonable and therefore not masters of a situation, but adult's emotions reasonable and allowed to govern. the confusion of restricted relationships is that we do not think other feelings e.g. desire for another's body, unreasonable, but just that those particular feelings are the ones to be controlled. the desire to possess and own takes precedence over other desires. (it is worth noting that this is particular to certain cultures and sexual jealousy is not comprehended in some. whilst it is "natural" for those of us raised in monogamous society to feel jealous, this does not mean those raised in polyamorous societies are just repressing their emotions!)
another key difference is that civilised society believes emotional growth occurs in childhood not adulthood. learning is not for life. this means the child can be given the opportunity to grow and develop but the adult is now retarded and incapable of learning

and this, brings us onto respect. coercive relationships are NOT respectful, for they are denial not only of desire but of growth. if i am bound by my lover's jealousy i presuppose them incapable of dealing with their emotions and too retarded to change. there is of course some truth in this. it is harder to be flexible at 30 than it is at 3. at 30 i have had 30 years of the megamachine and its myths of personal ownership. i have more shit to wade through, and i am likely to be hampered by well-meaning others trying not to "hurt" me. that hurt is just growing pains.

for someone to feel hurt by another it does not mean anyone has wronged anyone else. this is tricky land to negotiate but it is far from impossible. to openly accept feelings of jealousy and fear without asking or expecting another to restrict their behaviour thereby "solving" those feelings forces us to be the possessors not of another but of our own emotions. my hurt is my hurt. we can ask loved ones to love us through the hurt, and like the infant, we will probably find that hurt lessen and often leave. in particular, the victim culture of women – even amongst anarchists and feminists - is shackled by concepts that someone else is responsible for our feelings of rejection or upset. it is pitiful to blame our lovers for wanting someone else, even desiring someone else more than you, and even desiring someone else and not you.

BREAK OUT OR BREAK UP

due to our position of existing in mass society, and our needs to survive, some co- options and compromises are inevitable. our need to eat and have shelter makes us exploitative consumers, whether of "fair-trade" products or of pepperoni pizza. we are not connected with nature at any meaningful level even if we do grow our own vegetables in the "countryside". we all use technology to a greater or lesser degree. our relations meanwhile, are one of the places we are most free to try to be wild – to live in the here and now and without owning and oppressing each other.

to accept coercive relations as well as free ones is as full of folly as hoping industrial societies, or societies with governments, can exist alongside nature based ones. if my love is free, but yours is not then scarcity is created. to say i am at liberty to not possess land but you are at liberty to possess land is ludicrous. fortunately, your possession relies on my compliance with it, and as anarchists we do not accept your ownership and possession.

if we believe love should be freely given from desire then we cannot respect the culture of love-as-commodity-lover-as-possession.

> *" the middle person in the triangle often manifests a certain compassion for the suffering of the jealous one, respecting his "humanity" even though she regrets the unpleasant effects of misery's manipulations and melodramatics. this complicity remains loyal to the couple form, because it respects the traditional rules of love."*
> *Issac Cronin*

this means that for me to not act on my desiring in loving who i will when i will, is to be complicit in a system of coercion, of control and of ownership that i am opposed to. no, i do not and cannot, accept the rules of "your" relationship. in a free society we will not be asking for the consent of one person to sleep with another anymore than we would ask a father for the "right" to marry his daughter. and here and now, we can also live that out. to "respect" restrictive relationships is to uphold them.

DIRECT ACTION

would it be so controversial to call a war on monogamy? to seduce the lovers of the possessive? could we help those trapped by their timid jealousies to grow into freedom by "stealing" kisses from those forbidden lips in front of their terrified eyes?

if this shocks or offends you perhaps you should ask yourself why.

COMMUNITIES NOT COUPLES

rule relationships, and the acceptance of them, betrays an internalised hierarchy. the relationship of a couple is of greater value and worth than others in the community. it would be equally unrealistic and undesirable to hope for everyone to feel as much love and connection with every single one of their community – down that path lies formalised and institutionalised groups or other coercive ways of relating which are just as damaging as rule relationships and coupledom. community is more than one and it is more than two also. to create self-governing, self-sufficient small communities there cannot be the tyranny of individualism or of coupledom. to create wild and anarchistic communities we must also forsake the idea of sacrificing individual desires for the sake of the community. we have been so programmed by the megamachine that it is hard to imagine such a world where cooperation rather than competition does not elicit us as without. even harder to imagine is a world where we are free to take our pleasures and our desires openly. but if these are the communities we are in the process of creating then we must be honest and open and challenging. these communities will not prosper by shying from conflict but rather by not fearing it.

an argument often given by those who do not necessarily preach coercive relationships but are restricted by the ideology is this:

it is reasonable for A to not kiss B in front of C.

it is reasonable because A cares for C as much as she does for B.

A does not want to upset C.

nobody wants to upset those we care for. but if we restrict or inhibit our own desires for the false peace of not upsetting others, then we are left in a passionately deficit world. what then if C was upset because A and B were both female and C's masculinity was threatened by queer sex? or if C was upset because A was black and B was white and C's security as a black man was upset by mixed race love?

as radicals we would inevitably say the lovers should challenge homophobia and racism, that the onus is on C to deal with his feelings. and rightly so. homophobia and racism are internalised and damaging dynamics of control and power that must be challenged. so are rule relationships.

would you kiss B in front of C if C would be upset?!

RIGHT HERE, RIGHT NOW

the defining features of green anarchy include a desire to live in small, self-governing communities, individual and collective self-determination, a reconnection with the wild and an understanding that we live only in the present, in the here and now.

living in the real here and now instead of in the unreal past/future is a discerning feature of many nature based societies and one of the greatest poverties for us in mass society. dredging up dysfunctional childhoods or storing pensions for our old age deny us the being alive of the present. sitting in an office dreaming of the weekend or spending free time engaging with mythical soap opera characters instead of real people is clearly not healthy. equally unwell-making is having feelings incompatible with the here and now. sitting in the woods with a lover but being miserably occupied with something that happened as a child is the same as not enjoying a feast because once you had felt hungry.

the past is behind us. the future might never happen.

happiness is also located in the here and now, in the moment. we have spent our lives unlearning this but we catch glimpses of it through sex, love, pain, reunion, the unexpected etc. for our relations to be happy ones they must also be in the here and now, because, really, they only exist in the here and now. the famous quote "there is no such thing as heterosexuality and homosexuality, only heterosexual and homosexual acts" can be extended to realise that sexual unions are sexual only in that defining moment not the day before or the day after. it is delusional and painful to insist on consistent sexual desire, to demand your lover of today still loves you tomorrow.

gay, straight, my lover, your primary partner, it's all identity politics of ongoing contracts unbefitting to lives of mutual desires. we do not need to "work" at our relationships" merely have them. without contract, demand, competition and coercion

> *" i hate all those who, by ceding through fear and resignation, a part of their potential as human beings to others, not only crush themselves but also me and those i love, with the weight of their fearful complicity or with their idiotic inertia."*
>
> *(albert libertad – i hate the resigned)*

Text taken directly from a pamphlet published by Leeds Earth First!, 2004.

Resources

There are a number of interesting publications out there covering the issue of polyamory in various political aspects, or not at all.

One of the best short texts on open relationships is "With Open Hands" by Paxus / Fingerbook Project. http://www.twinoaks.org/members- exmembers/members/paxus/openhand.html

The original Green anarchist collection of texts is "Sexy uality" from the Godhaven Ink – online at http://www.scribd.com/doc/88904/sexyouality For hard copies visit http://www.godhaven.org.uk

Two good books on polyamory and opern relationshiops in general are "The Ethical Slut" by Dossie Easton & Ca therine Liszt[2] and "Opening Up" by Tristian Taormino.

A useful online introduction to the world of polyamory is the FAQ at www.faqs.org/faqs/polyamory/faq

2. Note from a contributor: The perspective of this book is very sex-focused rather than relationships/intimacy-focused. This trend in polyamory in America is leading to more success in raising awareness and bringing it mainstream as part of the cultural obsession with sex. European approaches, however, tend to be much less sex-focused, but achieve much less widespread publication as a result A lot of great work is still to be translated into English.

More in-depth stuff can be found at
www.polyamoryonline.org,
practicalpolyamory.com
&
www.polyamory.org.uk

About Us

Dysophia is an imprint for publishing pamphlets and 'zines exploring issues around green anarchist thought in a way that makes the issues accessible to everyone. We try to avoid dense theory, but give the knowledge to empower and make up your own minds.

For us green anarchism is a powerful tool for analysing much of the world around us, from interpersonal relationships to how we take on the big problems standing between us and our ideal society. We want to educate and encourage debate, to question everything then bring it together with solutions that take us forward. We are not interested in prolonged bickering over moot points, but celebrate our diversity and our common ambitions.

It is okay to challenge each other, it is okay to disagree. Knowledge does not have to be unified, but through honest, open discussion everyone can benefit and make up their minds.

We are always interested in feedback, suggestions of topics to cover or even ideas of articles you would like to write for us. We will try to respond to all emails, but we cannot promise that we will. As much as we like debate what we ideally want are responses and articles we can use in future publications.

Currently available issues are;
Green Anarchism: a political toolbox (Dysophia 0)
Polyamory: anarchist perspectives (Dysophia 1)
The Crisis of Crises Pt1: The Financial Crisis (CC1)
The Crisis of Crises Pt2: Peak Resources & Climate Change (CC2) Criticism without Critique: a Climate Camp reader (CCR)
Poverty, Privilege and Immigration (Dysophia 2)
Antisemitism and Anarchy (Dysophia 3)
Anarchist Debates on Pivilege (Dysophia 4)
What About the Rapists? (Dysophia 5)

For more information email dysophia.ga@gmail.com or write to Dysophia, c/o CRC, 16 Sholebroke Avenue, Leeds, LS7 3HB, UK

Copies of all our booklets can be found at ;

dysophia.org.uk

Dysophia are currently (2015 onwards) not publishing hard copies of texts as they are very involved with another important project. Active Distribution is gradually reprinting all the Dysophia texts as demand and our budget dictates! Find other Dysophia titles and much more besides at;

www.activedistribution.org